THE STANDARD FOR
PROGRAM MANAGEMENT

Fifth Edition

Library of Congress Cataloging-in-Publication Data

Names: Project Management Institute.
Title: The standard for program management / Project Management Insitute.
Description: Fifth edition. | Newtown Square, Pennsylvania : Project
    Management Institute, Inc., 2024. | Includes index. | Summary: "The
    Standard for Program Management - Fifth Edition identifies program
    management principles and performance domains and provides guidance on
    the principles of program management that guide the behaviors and
    actions of organizations, professionals, and stakeholders who work on or
    are engaged with programs. The standard provides generally accepted
    definitions of programs and program management as well as concepts
    important to their success: program management principles, performance
    domains, the program life cycle, practices, and supporting activities
    and tools. This fifth edition of The Standard for Program Management
    expands and clarifies concepts presented in previous editions. It
    complements and aligns with the Project Management Institute's (PMI)
    core foundational standards and guidance documents"-- Provided by
    publisher.
Identifiers: LCCN 2023054477 (print) | LCCN 2023054478 (ebook) | ISBN
    9781628258141 (paperback) | ISBN 9781628258158 (epub)
Subjects: LCSH: Project management--Standards.
Classification: LCC HD69.P75 S737 2024 (print) | LCC HD69.P75 (ebook) |
    DDC 658.4/04--dc23/eng/20231222
LC record available at https://lccn.loc.gov/2023054477
LC ebook record available at https://lccn.loc.gov/2023054478

ISBN: 978-1-62825-814-1

Published by:
    Project Management Institute, Inc.
    18 Campus Blvd., Ste. 150
    Newtown Square, Pennsylvania 19073-3299 USA
    PMI.org
    Phone: +1 610 356 4600
    Email: customercare@pmi.org

To place an order or for pricing information, please contact Independent Publishers Group:
    Independent Publishers Group
    Order Department
    814 North Franklin Street
    Chicago, IL 60610 USA
    Phone: 800 888 4741
    Fax: +1 312 337 5985
    Email: orders@ipgbook.com (For orders only)

10 9 8 7 6 5 4 3 2 1

Notice

The Project Management Institute, Inc. (PMI) standards and guideline publications, of which the document contained herein is one, are developed through a voluntary consensus standards development process. This process brings together volunteers and/or seeks out the views of persons who have an interest in the topic covered by this publication. While PMI administers the process and establishes rules to promote fairness in the development of consensus, it does not write the document and it does not independently test, evaluate, or verify the accuracy or completeness of any information or the soundness of any judgments contained in its standards and guideline publications.

PMI disclaims liability for any personal injury, property or other damages of any nature whatsoever, whether special, indirect, consequential or compensatory, directly or indirectly resulting from the publication, use of application, or reliance on this document. PMI disclaims and makes no guaranty or warranty, expressed or implied, as to the accuracy or completeness of any information published herein, and disclaims and makes no warranty that the information in this document will fulfill any of your particular purposes or needs. PMI does not undertake to guarantee the performance of any individual manufacturer or seller's products or services by virtue of this standard or guide.

In publishing and making this document available, PMI is not undertaking to render professional or other services for or on behalf of any person or entity, nor is PMI undertaking to perform any duty owed by any person or entity to someone else. Anyone using this document should rely on his or her own independent judgment or, as appropriate, seek the advice of a competent professional in determining the exercise of reasonable care in any given circumstances. Information and other standards on the topic covered by this publication may be available from other sources, which the user may wish to consult for additional views or information not covered by this publication.

PMI has no power, nor does it undertake to police or enforce compliance with the contents of this document. PMI does not certify, test, or inspect products, designs, or installations for safety or health purposes. Any certification or other statement of compliance with any health or safety-related information in this document shall not be attributable to PMI and is solely the responsibility of the certifier or maker of the statement.

Table of Contents

List of Figures and Tables

Introduction

The Standard for Program Management—Fifth Edition identifies program management principles and performance domains and provides guidance on the principles of program management that guide the behaviors and actions of organizations, professionals, and stakeholders who work on or are engaged with programs. The standard provides generally accepted definitions of programs and program management as well as concepts important to their success: program management principles, performance domains, the program life cycle, practices, and supporting activities and tools. This fifth edition of *The Standard for Program Management* expands and clarifies concepts presented in previous editions. It complements and aligns with the Project Management Institute's (PMI) core foundational standards and guidance documents, including *A Guide to the Project Management Body of Knowledge* (PMBOK® *Guide*) and *The Standard for Project Management* [1];[1] *Process Groups: A Practice Guide* [2]; *The Standard for Portfolio Management* [3]; *The Standard for Earned Value Management* [4]; *The Standard for Organizational Project Management* [5]; *The Standard for Risk Management in Portfolios, Programs, and Projects* [6]; *PMI Lexicon of Project Management Terms* [7]; *Governance of Portfolios, Programs, and Projects: A Practice Guide* [8]; *The Standard for Business Analysis* [9]; and *Benefits Realization Management: A Practice Guide* [10].

---

[1] The numbers in brackets refer to the list of references at the end of this standard.

This section defines and explains terms related to the standard's scope and provides an introduction to the content that follows. It includes the following major sections:

1.1 Purpose of *The Standard for Program Management*

1.2 What Is a Program?

1.3 What Is Program Management?

1.4 The Relationships among Organizational Strategy, Program Management, Portfolio Management, and Operations Management

1.5 Organizational Business Value

1.6 Role of the Program Manager

1.7 Role of the Program Sponsor

1.8 Role of the Program Management Office

1.9 Program and Project Distinctions

1.10 Portfolio and Program Distinctions

1.1 PURPOSE OF *THE STANDARD FOR PROGRAM MANAGEMENT*

The Standard for Program Management provides guidance on principles, practices, roles, and activities of program management that are generally recognized to support good program management practices and are applicable to most programs, most of the time.

▶ *Principles* of program management are fundamental norms, truths, or values. The principles for program management provide guidance for the behaviors and actions of people involved in programs as they influence and shape the performance domains to achieve intended benefits.

▶ *General consensus* means there is general agreement among the experts who produced this standard that the described principles, knowledge, and practices are valuable and useful.

▶ *Good practice* means there is general acceptance that the application of the principles, knowledge, and practices outlined in this standard will improve the management of programs and enhance the chances of program success, as measured by the extent and effectiveness of benefits delivery and realization. Good practice does not mean that all provisions of the standard are required to be applied to every program, as there is no one-sized fit for all. An organization's leaders, its program managers, its program teams, its value-and-benefits-realization management office, and its program management office (when one is employed) are responsible for determining what is most appropriate for any given program, based on the unique or specific requirements of the program and its sponsoring organization.

The Standard for Program Management is also intended to provide a common understanding of the role of a program manager in general, and especially when interacting with:

- Portfolio managers whose portfolios include the program or its components;

- Project managers whose projects or components are part of the program;

- Program steering committee (which may consist of technical partners or cosponsors that may provide cash or in-kind contribution to a program) that provides specialized inputs to the program manager, program advisory committee, management oversight committee, or program governance board;

- Portfolio, program, or project management office;

- Portfolio, program, or project team members working on the program or on other subsidiary programs;

- Program beneficiaries;

- Functional managers/groups and other subject matter experts (SMEs);

- Business analysis practitioners;

- Managers who are responsible for day-to-day organizational management who may be part of a program;

- C-level technical leadership, including chief product owners, chief product managers, head strategy and architecture, enterprise risk, organization change management, etc.;

- Strategy staff;

- Chief product owner and chief architecture owner;

- Other program managers who are part of subsidiary programs within a single program; and

- Other stakeholders or stakeholder groups (e.g., organizational executives, operations management, partners, product owners and managers, clients, suppliers, vendors, leaders, donors, end users, regulatory bodies, political groups, business owners, epic owners, enterprise architects, product managers, system architects) who may influence or be influenced by the program.

The Standard for Program Management is intended to be applied according to the *PMI Code of Ethics and Professional Conduct* [11], which specifies obligations of responsibility, accountability, respect, fairness, and honesty that program managers should abide by in the conduct of their work. The *PMI Code of Ethics and Professional Conduct* requires that practitioners demonstrate a commitment to ethical and professional conduct, and carries with it the obligation to comply with laws, regulations, and organizational and professional policies.

1.2 WHAT IS A PROGRAM?

A *program* comprises related projects, subsidiary programs, and program activities managed in a coordinated manner to obtain benefits not available from managing them individually. The components of a program are related through their pursuit of complementary goals that contribute to the delivery of benefits.

Managing program components enhances the delivery of benefits. It does so by ensuring that the strategies and work plans of program *components* are responsively and proactively adapted to component outcomes or to changes in the direction or strategies of the sponsoring organization. Programs are conducted primarily to deliver benefits to their target stakeholders, sponsor organizations, or constituents of the sponsoring organization. Programs deliver benefits, for example, by enhancing current capabilities, implementing change, creating or maintaining assets, offering new products and services, developing new opportunities to generate or preserve value, minimizing company loss or reputation damage, considering interrelated risk approaches, or implementing a minimal risk entry to a market or a minimal risk exit from a market. In the case of governments, programs can either provide services to beneficiaries or enforce obligations. Such benefits are delivered to the sponsoring organization as outcomes that provide value to the organization and the program's intended beneficiaries, target publics, or stakeholders.

Programs deliver their intended benefits primarily through components that are pursued to produce outputs and outcomes. Programs are typically executed over a longer period of time than projects—although not always—and their outcomes may span multiple phases, cycles, and organizations. Therefore, program management requires a holistic and systemic approach, governing activities as well as a long-term perspective.

Component projects, subsidiary programs, or programs that do not advance common or complementary goals; do not jointly contribute to the delivery of common benefits; and/or are related only by common sources of support, technology, or stakeholders are often better managed as portfolios rather than as programs (see *The Standard for Portfolio Management* [3]). It is important to clarify that the concept of the program is not always related to the size of the work but depends on the type of relations between its components and the program benefits provided by the integration of the project relationship.

The following is a list of program components and their definitions:

▶ *Components* are projects, subsidiary programs, or other related activities conducted to support a program.

▶ *Projects* are temporary endeavors undertaken to create a unique product, service, or result, as described fully in *A Guide to the Project Management Body of Knowledge* (*PMBOK® Guide*) [1]. Projects are used to generate the outcomes required by programs and/or portfolios, within defined constraints such as budget, time, scope, risks, resources, and quality, to create value for the organization.

▶ *Subsidiary programs* are programs sponsored and conducted to pursue a subset of goals and benefits important to the primary program. As an example, a program to develop a new electric car may sponsor other subsidiary programs related to the development of new motor, battery, and charging station technologies. Each of these subsidiary programs would be managed as described in this standard and also monitored and managed as a component of the primary program.

▶ *Other program-related activities* are work processes or activities that are being conducted to support a program but are not directly tied to the subsidiary programs or projects sponsored or conducted by a program. Examples of processes and activities sponsored by programs may include those related to training, planning, program-level control, reporting, accounting, auditing, stakeholder engagement, and administration. Operational activities or maintenance functions that are directly related to a program's components may be considered as other program-related activities or part of operations work itself. For example, the program would typically include a project to create the assembly line for the electric car. Running that assembly line once it is built falls under the scope of operations, not the program, which runs during a defined timeframe.

When used in the context of program management, the term *activities* should be read as *program activities*. Program activities are activities conducted to support a program, and not those activities performed during the course of a program's components. The other program-related activities, needs, structure, management, and good practices should be followed to establish correct governance structure, in order to avoid placing extra burdens on program managers.

The best mechanism for delivering a program's benefits may initially be ambiguous or uncertain. Outcomes delivered by a program's components contribute to the delivery of the program's intended benefits and, as necessary, to refinement of the strategy of the program and its components.

The primary purpose of a program is to achieve the organization's strategy in order to deliver tangible/intangible and short-/long-term benefits and values. Thus, the value of managing an initiative as a program results from the program manager's readiness to align and adapt strategies to optimize the delivery of benefits to an organization. As a consequence of a program's potential need to adapt to the outcomes of its components, and its potential need to modify its strategy or plans, program components may be pursued in an incremental, iterative, and nonsequential manner.

The program life cycle, depicted in Figure 1-1, illustrates the nonsequential nature of a program's life cycle phase. Program benefits may be identified throughout the duration of the program. The program life cycle is discussed in greater detail in Section 3.8 of this standard.

One example of a program that delivers benefits incrementally is an organization-wide process improvement program. Such a program might be envisioned to pursue component projects to standardize and consolidate specific processes (e.g., financial control processes, inventory management processes, hiring processes, performance appraisal processes) and subsidiary programs to ensure that the benefits of consolidation are fully realized (e.g., to ensure adoption of the improved processes or to measure employee satisfaction and performance with the new processes). Each of these components may deliver incremental benefits when completed. Another example of a program that delivers benefits incrementally is an infrastructure development program (such as roads, water) since the outcomes of the project are used once they are finished and start delivering benefits.

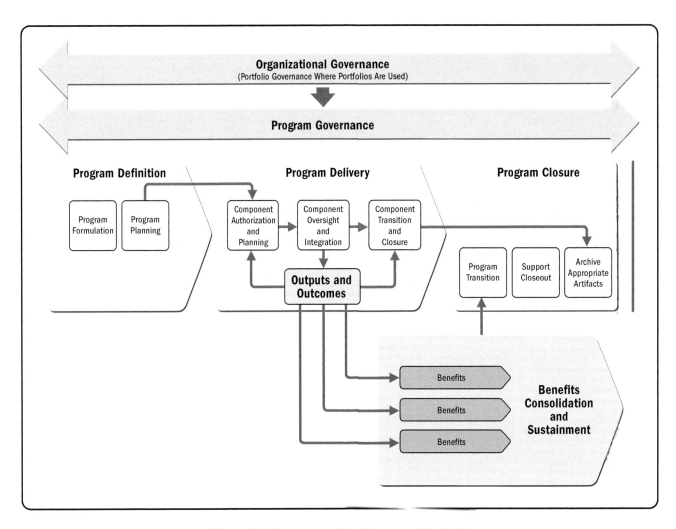

Figure 1-1. Representative Program Life Cycle

The outputs or outcomes of components might trigger the initiation of new projects to further improve and optimize existing processes, or modify or terminate current projects, which may lead to improved performance of the existing projects or the program as a whole, thus enhancing processes, stakeholder satisfaction, and performance. The program, however, would not be considered as complete until all of the projects and subsidiary programs necessary for business improvement have delivered their intended program benefits. It is important to remember that new improvement projects are linked to program goals. In addition, as business cycle improvement is constant—despite any changes—it is essential to consider the importance of the linkage between program objectives for success and new projects. Benefits should be measurable and linked to the outcome of the project, portfolio, or strategy.

Alternatively, programs may deliver intended benefits all at once, as a unified whole. In this case, the benefits of the program are not realized until the program is completed. A drug development program can be considered as a program with unified benefits delivery, where the individual components of the program would not be expected to deliver benefits until the entire drug development program is successfully completed, the product is tested and approved, patients are treated with it, and the organization realizes benefits from its production. The working relationship between the program manager and the operations team is critical to this process in order to ensure monitoring and proper handover, benefits realization, and program sustainability.

1.2.1 INITIATION OF PROGRAMS

Programs are generally initiated or recognized in two ways: a top-down approach or a bottom-up approach.

▶ **Top-down approach.** Programs initiated to pursue new goals, objectives, or strategies are begun before the start of work on their component projects and programs. These programs are typically initiated to support and align with strategic goals and objectives; they enable an organization to pursue its vision and mission. Examples of such programs include programs initiated as part of an organization's strategic planning process (such as part of a portfolio-based decision to develop a new product, service, or result, or to expand into a new market), to influence human behavior (such as to raise awareness of desired behaviors or to ensure compliance with new regulations), or to respond to a crisis (e.g., to provide disaster relief or manage a public health issue). These programs are generally supported from the beginning by program activities. Programs are initiated inside portfolios where they exist. Where portfolios are not present, programs may inherit some of the characteristics of a portfolio, and the role and responsibilities of the managing program manager are correspondingly modified. To learn more about this, see Section 1.9 of this document or refer to *The Standard for Portfolio Management* [3].

▶ **Bottom-up approach.** Programs may be formed when an organization recognizes that its ongoing activities, which may be associated with projects, programs, and/or other work, are related/interdependent by their pursuit of common outcomes, capabilities, objectives, or benefits (e.g., a process improvement program supported by previously independent software development initiatives or a neighborhood revitalization program supported by building public parks, developing traffic control projects, and establishing a community outreach program). These programs are often formed when an organization determines that organizational benefits would be more effectively realized by managing ongoing initiatives as a single program. Such programs are supported by program activities after some or all of their projects have been initiated.

Programs may also be initiated for the following reasons: to make a positive impact on society, such as promoting sustainability, supporting community development, supporting resilience activities, improving public health, or enhancing public infrastructure (water, sanitation, roads); to encourage and support innovation, whether it's through research and development, new product launches, or exploring new technologies; or to help organizations adapt to the digital age, whether it's through adoption of new technologies, developing new digital products and services, or modernizing existing processes.

Newly initiated or identified programs should all be managed according to the principles (see Section 2) and life cycle management guidance (see Section 3.8) described in the subsequent sections of this standard. It is incumbent on a program manager to ensure, for example, that activities important to program definition be completed for programs whose projects and other programs may have already begun.

1.2.2 THE RELATIONSHIPS AMONG PORTFOLIOS, PROGRAMS, OPERATIONS, AND PROJECTS

The relationships among portfolios, programs, and projects are as follows:

- A *portfolio* is a collection of projects, programs, subsidiary portfolios, and operations managed as a group to achieve strategic objectives.

- *Programs* consist of a group of related projects, subsidiary programs, and program activities managed in a coordinated manner to obtain benefits and outcomes not available from managing them individually. Programs are often common elements of portfolios, conducted to deliver benefits and value important to an organization's strategic objectives.

- *Projects*, whether they are managed independently or as part of a program or portfolio, are endeavors undertaken to create unique products, services, or results, delivering value for the organization.

Programs and projects may be significant elements of an organization's portfolio structure and are conducted to produce the outcomes required to create the desired benefits and support an organization's strategic objectives. These could be altered or terminated if there is a change to the sponsor's strategy or organizational priorities.

Figure 1-2 illustrates how portfolios, programs, and projects fit into an example value delivery system. It illustrates an example of how various components are placed under a portfolio structure.

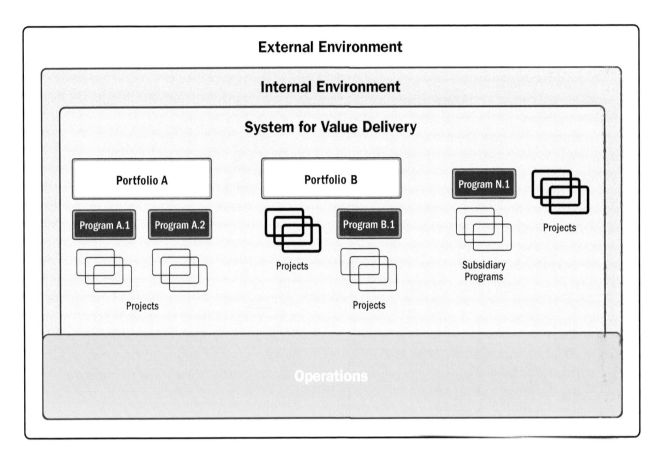

Figure 1-2. Components of an Example Value Delivery System

Various components can be used individually and collectively to create benefits and value. Working collaboratively, these components comprise a system of delivery that is aligned with the organization's strategy. Figure 1-2 gives an example of a system for value delivery that has two portfolios composed of programs and projects. It also presents a stand-alone program with projects and stand-alone projects not associated with portfolios, programs, products, services, or results. Any of the projects or programs could include products. A program life cycle generally is longer than a project life cycle and may consist of an entire program or portfolio, depending on management structure. Operations can directly support, be a part of, or influence portfolios, programs, and projects, as well as other business functions.

Figure 1-3 shows a system for value delivery in part of an organization's internal environment and its component information flows, which are subject to policies, procedures, methodologies, frameworks, governance structure, and so forth.

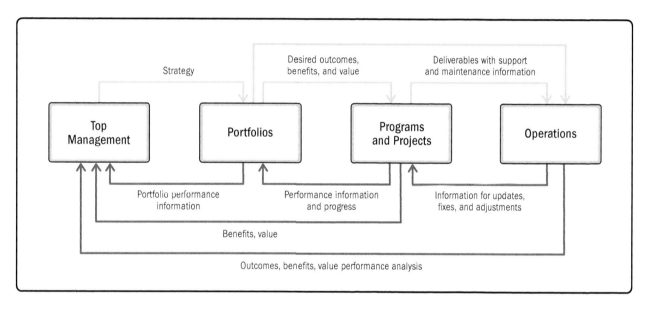

Figure 1-3. Example Information Flow in a System for Value Delivery

1.3 WHAT IS PROGRAM MANAGEMENT?

Program management is the application of knowledge, skills, and principles to a program to achieve the program objectives and to obtain benefits and control not available by managing program components individually. It involves aligning program components and resources to ensure that program goals are met, benefits are optimally delivered, and risks are effectively managed. Program management is led by a *program manager*, who is the person authorized by the performing organization to lead the team or teams responsible for achieving program objectives.

The program manager provides the effective alignment, integration, and control of the program's components (projects, subsidiary programs, and program activities) by actions taken in six interrelated and interdependent program management performance domains:

▶ Strategic Alignment

▶ Benefits Management

▶ Stakeholder Engagement

▶ Governance Framework

▶ Collaboration

▶ Life Cycle Management

Program management performance domains are complementary groupings of related areas of activity or function that uniquely characterize and differentiate the activities found in one performance domain from the others within the full scope of program management work. These performance domains are discussed in detail in subsequent sections of this standard. Through these program management performance domains, the program manager oversees and analyzes interdependencies to determine the optimal approach for managing program components. Actions related to these interdependencies may include:

▶ Align various project management approaches and methodologies among projects within a program (e.g., predictive, agile, adaptive, hybrid, etc.).

▶ Define how the outcomes of a program's components are expected to contribute to the program's delivery of its intended benefits and resulting value, as well as support the organization's strategy.

▶ Plan the targeted benefits to be delivered partially in iterations throughout the program life cycle when using an incremental delivery approach, e.g., agile.

The Standard for Program Management

- ▶ Monitor benefits realization of program components to ensure they remain strategically aligned to the organization's objectives.

- ▶ Ensure that the outcomes of a program's components are considered and communicated to the appropriate stakeholders, so that the program can effectively optimize the pursuit of its intended benefits and provide value.

- ▶ Lead, coordinate, and collaborate on program activities (e.g., financing and procurement) across all program components, work, or phases.

- ▶ Communicate with and report to the program sponsor(s) and other key stakeholders to provide an integrated, collaborative perspective on appropriate program management activities being pursued within the program.

- ▶ Assess risks and proactively take action, spanning all components of the program.

- ▶ Ensure adherence to the program roadmap.

- ▶ Align program efforts with the organizational strategy and the program's business case.

- ▶ Resolve scope, cost, schedule, resources, quality, benefits, communications, procurement, stakeholders, and risk issues within the shared governance structure.

- ▶ Tailor program activities, processes, and interfaces to address cultural, socioeconomic, political, and environmental differences within the program.

- ▶ Ensure the component's outcomes are scheduled to be delivered in the precise moment while considering business-specific needs and optimizing resources.

- ▶ Participate with, guide, and direct program component managers on the methodologies and approaches used in managing their projects within the program.

- ▶ Perform comprehensive dependencies management.

- ▶ Integrate program benefits.

- ▶ Lead and participate in developing an integrated program framework to facilitate collaboration among subprograms, projects, and operations based upon the components' unique approaches and needs.

Program managers apply program management principles to ensure that programs and their components are planned, managed, controlled, and completed, and that program benefits are appropriately delivered and sustained through interface management.

1.4 THE RELATIONSHIPS AMONG ORGANIZATIONAL STRATEGY, PROGRAM MANAGEMENT, PORTFOLIO MANAGEMENT, AND OPERATIONS MANAGEMENT

Organizations apply program management to pursue complex initiatives that support organizational strategy. In practice, when pursuing such initiatives, program managers also find that their programs impact lines of business with operational responsibilities. Moreover, program managers often find that the benefits delivered by programs may influence an organization's approach to, or scope of, operational activities, and that the program's component deliverables are transferred to organizational entities to ensure that their delivery of benefits is sustained. For these reasons, it is important that program managers establish collaborative, mutually supportive relationships with those responsible for managing operations within an organization. Together, program and operational managers are responsible for the balanced and successful execution of an organization's strategic objectives.

Depending on the change management maturity of the organization, the program manager may find the function of a change management office useful. This office can help the program manager integrate the change management activities with project/program activities, in order to reach a smooth transition of the outcomes to the operations teams and to ensure the sustainability of the change. Sometimes the program manager must also be ready to perform change management activities if there is no dedicated change management professional or office. Understanding how to identify the current maturity level of an organization and the steps needed to navigate its unique environment are essential skills.

Organizations address the need for change by creating strategic business initiatives to produce results or change the organization, its products, or its services. Portfolios of programs and projects are the vehicles for delivering these initiatives. For more information on the use of programs to produce change, see *Managing Change in Organizations: A Practice Guide* [12].

1.5 ORGANIZATIONAL BUSINESS VALUE

Organizations employ program management to improve their abilities to deliver benefits and increase and maintain value for the organization and its target audiences. In noncommercial organizations, benefits can be delivered in the form of social, societal, or organizational value (e.g., improved health, safety, or security). In commercial organizations, it is common for organizational benefits to be delivered in the form of organizational value. Organizational value may be defined as the sum of all tangible and intangible elements of an organization that contribute to their purpose or vision. For example, tangible elements include monetary assets, facilities, fixtures, equity, tools, market share, sustainable development, and utility. Intangible elements may include goodwill, brand recognition, public benefit, trademarks, compliance, reputation, strategic alignment, and capabilities. Organizational value may also be created through the execution of strategic goals and ongoing, well-established operations. However, the use of portfolio, program, and project management as part of the organization's system of value delivery enables the organization to employ reliable, established principles and processes to generate new value through the pursuit of new strategies consistent with its mission and vision for the future.

Portfolio management ensures that an organization's programs, projects, and operations are aligned with its strategy. It allows organizations to define how they will pursue their strategic goals through programs and projects, and how those programs and projects will be supported by human, financial, technical, or material resources. These portfolio management efforts should help optimize the pursuit of organizational value.

Program management enables organizations to pursue their strategic goals through the coordinated pursuit of projects, subsidiary programs, and other program-related activities. Program management seeks to optimize the management of related component projects and programs to improve the generation of organizational value. Program management balances the program throughout its life cycle, enabling the program to sustainably realize planned benefits and deliver expected value. Also, program management may help in one way or another to utilize the resources effectively and jointly between the components.

Project management enables organizations to more efficiently and effectively generate outcomes required for the pursuit of an organization's objectives by applying knowledge, processes, principles, skills, tools, and techniques that enhance the delivery of outcomes by projects. Project management seeks to optimize the delivery of benefits and value by improving the efficiency of organizations as they deliver new products, services, or results.

1.6 ROLE OF THE PROGRAM MANAGER

A program manager is assigned by a senior official in the performing organization in accordance with the organization's governance procedures, and is authorized to lead the team (or teams of teams) responsible for delivering benefits and value. The program manager maintains the accountability and responsibility for the leadership, conduct, and performance of a program, and for building a program team that is capable of achieving program objectives and delivering anticipated program benefits and value. The role of the program manager is different from that of a project manager. The differences between these roles are based on the fundamental differences between programs and projects and between program management and project management as described in Sections 1.2 through 1.3. If the program is not governed by portfolio management, the program manager will need to assess which principles and performance domains from *The Standard for Portfolio Management* [3] (and their value and benefits) should be incorporated into the program activities.

In programs, the best means of delivering value and benefits (via projects, subsidiary programs, and other activities) may be uncertain at the beginning of the program. However, a program manager needs to improve the visibility of such means as the program progresses. The outcomes generated by the components of programs may be complex and unpredictable at times. As a consequence, programs should be managed to recognize the potential need to seek synergies and economies of scale among program components, and adapt strategies and plans during the course of a program to optimize the delivery of benefits and value. A primary role of the program manager is to proactively manage delivery execution to ensure continuous alignment with committed outcomes. Program managers should ensure that program components are adapted as required and that the program is continuously aligned with the organization's strategic objectives to deliver its planned benefits.

The program manager is also responsible for managing or coordinating the management of complex risks and issues that may arise as programs seek to deliver benefits. Such issues may result from uncertainties related to outcomes, operations, organizational strategies, resourcing, the external environment, the governance landscape, or the expectations and motivations of program stakeholders. Program managers must manage dependencies between projects.

The eight program management principles, six program management performance domains, and supporting program activities described in Sections 3.3 through 3.8 discuss the practices and program management skills required for navigating volatility, uncertainty, complexity, and ambiguity (i.e., navigating a VUCA environment), as well as for implementing change in the program environment to optimize the delivery of program benefits. These sections describe a framework and the principles for engaging stakeholders and steering committees, and for managing the progression of a program's life cycle. Section 4 identifies the core and supporting program activities recommended to facilitate the delivery of benefits.

In general, program managers are expected to:

▶ Exercise critical thinking skills while working within the eight program management principles and six program management performance domains.

▶ Collaborate with project and other program managers to provide support and guidance on individual initiatives conducted to support a program.

▶ Collaborate with portfolio managers to ensure that programs are provisioned with the appropriate resources based on their capability and capacity needs.

▶ Collaborate with governance bodies, sponsors, and the program management office, where applicable, to ensure the program's continued alignment with organizational strategy and ongoing organizational support. This is also critical to ensuring the compliance of the program components with the project management methodology set by the program management office, as well as compliance with local laws, regulations, and standards.

▶ Coordinate with operational managers and stakeholders (both internal and external) to ensure that programs receive appropriate operational support, and that benefits delivered by the program can be sustained.

▶ Ensure the scope and deliverables of each of a program's components are recognized and well understood by stakeholders and the program team.

▶ Ensure the optimum utilization of common resources between the program components. This role involves strategically planning and overseeing resource allocation among the various projects under a program to achieve maximum efficiency and effectiveness.

- Ensure the overall program structure is balanced and that the applied program management processes enable the program and its component teams to successfully complete the work and deliver anticipated benefits.

- Integrate the program components' deliverables, outcomes, and benefits into the program's end products, services, or results, such that the program is positioned to deliver its intended benefits.

- Transition the outcomes of the program and support the benefits realization process throughout the program's life cycle.

- Ensure that beneficiaries and stakeholders clearly understand how they will contribute to, or be affected by, the program and its intended outcomes and benefits.

- Nurture social awareness and support within the organization for the program's objectives throughout the program's life cycle to improve the program's ability to succeed and meet its intended goals.

- Act as the steward of the program to ensure the program meets its chartered objectives as efficiently and sustainably as possible.

- Provide effective and appropriate leadership and direction to the program and component teams.

- Engage the internal and external stakeholders (especially those belonging to government and who work as regulators) and manage their expectations following the most effective communications management plans and stakeholder engagement skills.

- Ensure that component projects and program schedules are synchronized, recognizing that changes or delays in one process may affect other program components' results, including the need for replanning.

- Provide robust vertical and horizontal communications across the program and its stakeholders.

In addition to the responsibilities already listed, program managers may also be expected to ensure that components, other programs, and program activities are organized and executed in a consistent manner and fulfilled within the established standards. Program managers also coordinate and synchronize the resources, especially the key interrelated resources among the program components and projects, to ensure the success of the projects. The program manager owns the overall success of the program on behalf of the organization and its leadership. The program manager is also accountable to the program sponsor and is responsible for the planning, execution, and overall management of the program, while implementing the organizational project management (OPM) standards, methodologies, processes, tools, and techniques, as applicable.

1.6.1 PROGRAM MANAGER COMPETENCIES

Program managers need to encourage the efficient completion of component, project, and other program activities as planned, while simultaneously enabling the adjustment of the strategy or plans of a program or its components whenever it will improve delivery of the program's intended benefits. Balancing these needs requires that program managers be competent in providing an integrated view of how the outcomes of program components will support the program's intended delivery of organizational benefits.

The expertise required of a program manager depends, to a large degree, on the proficiencies required to navigate the volatility, uncertainty, complexity, ambiguity, transformation, and change associated with a program's outcomes or environment. The skills required may differ significantly among programs of different types, or even among programs of similar types facing dissimilar challenges. They may, for example, include technical skills specific to the program's targeted outcomes, business skills specific to the program's environment, or advanced project management skills critical to the management of complex operational challenges. The following power skills and business acumen are commonly required of program managers. However, it is important to note that, although in some cases the skill set may vary depending on the program, a program manager with a general understanding and possession of these skills and competencies can successfully lead any type of program:

▶ **Communication and negotiation skills.** Communication and negotiation skills that enable effective exchange of information with a wide variety of program stakeholders, including program team members, sponsors, customers, vendors, and senior management, whether individually or in groups or committees.

▶ **Stakeholder engagement skills.** Stakeholder engagement skills to support the need to manage the complex issues that often arise as a consequence of stakeholder interactions. The program manager should recognize the dynamic aspects of managing individual and group expectations.

▶ **Change management skills**. Change management skills that enable effective engagement with individual stakeholders and governance and review committees to gain the necessary agreements, alignment, and approvals when program strategies or plans need to be adapted. The program manager should provide an integrated view of the perspectives of stakeholders and committees whenever a program interacts with multiple committees as part of an organization's program review and approval process.

▶ **Leadership and management skills.** These skills guide program teams throughout the program life cycle. Program managers work with component managers, and often with operational managers, to gain support, resolve conflicts, delegate responsibilities, and empower and direct individual program team members to do their jobs by providing work instructions as needed. This facilitates a systems thinking approach when solving problems with the program processes.

▶ **Collaboration and facilitation skills.** Collaboration and facilitation skills that enable effective teamwork and partnership management and enhance stakeholder support and engagement. These skills enable the program manager to navigate the motivations of various groups' interests in a program, resolve conflicts, achieve compromises, acquire resources, manage risks realistically, and meet compliance requirements, all while ensuring the program stays balanced throughout its life cycle to deliver upon its expected outcomes and benefits.

▶ **Analytical skills.** Analytical skills that enable a program manager to assess whether the outcomes of program components will contribute as expected to the delivery of program benefits, comprehend and manage the challenges and opportunities encountered by the program, or assess the potential impact of internal and external risks and issues on the program's strategy or plans. Critical thinking skills are very important.

▶ **Integration skills.** Integration skills that enable a program manager to describe and present a program's strategic vision and plan holistically. It is the program manager's responsibility to ensure the continuous alignment of the program component plans with the program's goals and pursuit of organizational benefits.

▶ **Business and strategic management skills.** Business skills that can enable the program benefits to be aligned to organizational strategy and the vision that helps program managers deal with uncertainties and the leadership interface. Business skills help translate benefit impacts and success to sponsors and foster more cohesive communications with the team.

▶ **Systems thinking skills.** Systems thinking skills that use adaptive and holistic management approaches and analysis techniques to address complexity within the program environment. Analysis techniques may include nonlinear, Monte Carlo, or multidimensional approaches.

▶ **Risk management skills.** Such skills encompass the ability to identify, analyze, plan for, and respond to potential risks in a program. This includes developing systematic processes for managing risk, making informed decisions under uncertainty, and designing contingency plans.

Skilled program managers who possess knowledge and experience in the program's area of focus generally will have an advantage over program managers who lack business-specific experience. Regardless of background, however, the successful program manager uses knowledge, experience, and leadership effectively to align the program's approach with the organization's strategy, improve the delivery of program benefits, enhance collaboration with stakeholders and program steering committees, and manage the program life cycle. In general, this requires the program manager to exhibit certain competences, including the abilities to:

▶ Manage details while taking a holistic, benefits-focused view of the program.

▶ Leverage a strong working knowledge of the principles, practices, processes, tools, methodologies, approaches, and techniques of portfolio, program, and project management.

▶ Interact seamlessly and collaboratively with program steering committees and other executive stakeholders.

▶ Establish productive and collaborative relationships with team members and their organizational stakeholders.

▶ Adapt to operational and strategic changes in the program's internal and external environments.

▶ Leverage business knowledge, skills, and experience to provide perspectives that support the understanding and navigation of volatility, uncertainty, complexity, and ambiguity (VUCA) in the program environment.

▶ Facilitate awareness, understanding, and agreement through the use of strong communication and negotiation skills.

Demonstrating these abilities within the context of a particular program or organization may present unique challenges. A program that has many technical or design issues may require a program manager with a technical background. On the other hand, a program that has many personnel and stakeholder coordination issues may require a program manager with an extensive background in managing collaborative relationships within contentious or antagonistic management environments. Self-aware program managers know their strengths and weaknesses and build a program management team that is complementary to their skill set.

Given the often complex and dynamic nature of programs, it is understandable that program managers may enter the field from the project management field or from a technical discipline closely related to their programs. Regardless of their path of entry to the field, program managers commonly seek specific development and training opportunities related to the key competences associated with the program manager role, such as the PMI Program Management Professional (PgMP)® certification program or other certifications, or through post-graduate academic study.

For additional information regarding program management competences, refer to the *Project Manager Competency Development Framework* [13].

1.7 ROLE OF THE PROGRAM SPONSOR

A program sponsor is an individual or group from a performing organization that provides resources and strategic support for the program and is accountable for enabling success. A program steering committee may assume the responsibilities of a program sponsor or senior manager, but this is uncommon and against good practices. The program sponsor is usually part of an organization's top management and is an individual who is committed to ensuring that the program is appropriately supported and able to deliver its intended benefits. In this capacity, the sponsor may support and assist the program manager in stakeholder engagement among other activities.

The program sponsor plays a key role in ensuring the program manager and program team clearly and unambiguously understand the goals and objectives for which the program is being chartered. In addition, the program sponsor also assists the program manager and program team with the definition of the benefits and outcomes of the program based on the portfolio or organizational needs. The program sponsor provides oversight and guidance for the program management plan so that benefits planning is aligned with the organization's strategic goals.

The program sponsor works to gain and sustain organizational buy-in for the program throughout its life cycle, so the program has a higher probability of success. Sponsors work collaboratively with funding organizations, third-party sponsors (such as the World Bank or Asian Development Bank), and other financial institutions to secure funding. The program sponsor also provides valuable guidance and support to the program manager, ensuring that the program receives appropriate high-level attention and consideration, and that the program manager is informed of organizational changes that may affect the program. The program sponsor has a major role in supporting the program by securing the funding and other resources for the approved program business case. It is also important to remember that the roles of the program sponsor and program steering committee are distinct and different. While it is possible for the program steering committee to act as program sponsor, this should only be done on a limited-time basis. The governance and management-focused roles of the program sponsor are discussed in more detail in Sections 3.5.1 and 3.6.2.1, respectively.

1.8 ROLE OF THE PROGRAM MANAGEMENT OFFICE

A program management office is an organizational management structure, usually internal to the program management's organization. It is responsible for supporting assigned programs and improving program management maturity within its organization. The program management office standardizes program-related governance processes and facilitates the sharing of resources, methodologies, tools, and techniques. A program management office also supports training, quality assurance activities, and organizational process improvement activities. The specific role of a program management office is varied based upon organizational needs, governance structure, resources, and the organization's general program management approach or philosophy.

Depending upon the type of organization, the organization's mission and structure, and the organization's execution of process to achieve its goals, the program management office may take different forms and structures. For example, some organizations may use "project management office" as an umbrella term that is inclusive of project, program, and portfolio management offices or functions. Labels may vary by organization. An organization may also have more than one program management office, including a hierarchical structure.

Program management offices may be established within an individual program to provide support specific to that program, or independent of an individual program to provide support to one or more of an organization's programs (for more detail, see Sections 3.5.1 and 3.6.2.3, respectively). When established as part of a program, a program management office is an important element of the program's infrastructure and an aid to the program manager. It may support the program manager with the management of multiple projects and program activities, for example, by:

▶ Defining standard program management processes, policies, and procedures that should be followed;

▶ Developing and managing program management methodology, good practices, quality assurance activities, or standards;

▶ Developing and managing program management documents;

▶ Providing mentoring and training to ensure that standards and practices are understood;

- ▶ Supporting program communications;

- ▶ Supporting program-level change management activities;

- ▶ Conducting program performance analyses;

- ▶ Supporting management of the program scope, schedule, and budget;

- ▶ Monitoring delivery of expected benefits, results, or outcomes;

- ▶ Supporting a smooth transfer of benefits from the program level to the operations level to sustain and realize those benefits;

- ▶ Defining general quality standards for the program and its components;

- ▶ Supporting effective resource management;

- ▶ Providing support for reporting to leadership and program steering committees;

- ▶ Supporting document and knowledge transfer; and

- ▶ Providing centralized support for managing changes and tracking risks, issues, and decisions.

In addition, for large or complex programs, the program management office may provide additional management support for personnel and other resources, contracts and procurements, and legal or legislative issues.

Some programs continue for years and assume many aspects of normal operations that overlap with the larger organization's operational management. The program management office may take on some of these responsibilities. The specific governance and management-focused roles of the program management office are described further in Sections 3.6 and 4, respectively.

Some organizations opt not to have formally defined program management offices. In those instances, the managing function of the program management office is generally assumed by the assigned program manager.

1.9 PROGRAM AND PROJECT DISTINCTIONS

Program management provides organizations with a framework for managing interrelated groupings of work (e.g., projects, subsidiary programs, and program activities) designed to produce benefits not determined to be achievable by managing the work as individual initiatives. This section further discusses three characteristics that distinguish programs from projects, namely, uncertainty, change, and complexity. Where programs are not present, projects may inherit some of the characteristics of programs and, in some cases, portfolios.

As discussed in Section 1.2.2, it is important to remember:

▶ Programs consist of a group of related projects, subsidiary programs, and program activities managed in a coordinated manner to obtain benefits and outcomes not available from managing them individually. Programs are often common elements of portfolios, conducted to deliver benefits and value important to an organization's strategic objectives.

▶ Projects, whether they are managed independently or as part of a program or portfolio, are endeavors undertaken to create unique products, services, or results, delivering value for the organization.

1.9.1 UNCERTAINTY

Risk permeates both the program and project management environments. Impacts vary regarding the specific project or program. The common denominator, however, is uncertainty. Uncertainty is a fundamental attribute that may be a cause or result of complexity in both programs and projects. Program and project organizational structures are set up to facilitate monitoring (mitigating whenever possible) and controlling (to the extent possible) of risks and related uncertainties.

Projects and programs are distinguished by the level and authority associated with their management structures. Project management structures are taken to be at a lower level within the organization than program management structures. While risk tolerance and appetite may drive an individual manager's response to risk, risk management at the project level tends to be more conservative, with an emphasis on risk reduction in response to threats.

Projects, compared to programs, may also be limited in their ability to take advantage of opportunities because of resource and oversight limitations. The project team's ability to respond to opportunities is usually more limited than at the program level because of resource limitations and the additional oversight within a governing program or portfolio management office, if in place.

Project success is usually measured by delivery of a product in terms of value, timeliness, budget, and customer satisfaction and the value derived therein. Program success, although dependent on the delivery of its projects' products, services, or results, is measured by the delivery of benefits to an organization in an effective and efficient manner. Both projects and programs seek to deliver benefits and quality to the customer. However, the focus, as outlined above, is significantly different for projects and programs.

As such, the project's handling of uncertainty is within the context of successful delivery of an end item or service. This perspective is usually driven by tactical considerations and typically results in management approaches that seek to minimize uncertainty throughout the project life cycle. Management practices such as progressive elaboration are used, but usually as tools to minimize uncertainty. Even within agile approaches such as Scrum, Extreme Programming (XP), and Scaled Agile Framework (SAFe®), uncertainty is minimized using a short delivery time horizon (sprints, if using Scrum, are typically 1–2 weeks).

At the program level, the approach to uncertainty is different, primarily because programs focus on delivering benefits, not products. Usually, longer timeframes associated with a program life cycle—and the program management team's position at a higher level within the organization—also contribute to how uncertainty is viewed. As such, individuals at the program level tend to have broader management views, more authority, and additional information that may not be available at lower levels of management. Program-level managers are usually better equipped to handle more risk and are able to embrace uncertainty as a tool to enhance program opportunities within their organization's overall strategic goals. The program team is also in a better position to mitigate threats. Additionally, being higher in the organization's management chain, the program team works under fewer layers of management and is usually better connected to senior corporate staff.

The above factors tend to drive the project team to management actions that minimize uncertainty and risks, in general. However, at the program level, due to greater management authority and a wider vision, uncertainty may be embraced more as a tool to drive opportunities or to find ways, unavailable at the project level, to avoid or mitigate risks and the associated uncertainties.

1.9.2 MANAGING CHANGE

Program managers need to consider three different categories of change: program, internal change, and external change. A program is a change process in itself, and the program manager must be familiar with change methodologies in order to deliver value to the organization. Internal change refers to shifts within a program. External change refers to changes in the overall business environment, either within or outside of the program organization.

Risks and issues related to change should be addressed differently within programs and projects. In both programs and projects, there should be a rationale justifying that the advantages originating from a proposed change will outweigh any potential drawbacks. Change within a project affects the defined deliverables at the tactical level, whereas change within a program affects the delivery of the intended benefits at the strategic and tactical level. Managing change within a program requires strategic insight, knowledge, and an understanding of the program's objectives and intended benefits. Change to any component within a program may have a direct impact on the delivery of the other related components, which necessitates a change in those specific components.

In programs, change management is a key activity, enabling stakeholders to carefully analyze the need for a proposed change, the impact of the change, and the approach or process for implementing and communicating that change. The change management mechanism, which is part of the program management plan and developed during program planning, establishes the change management authorities.

▶ **Program change.** Change management programs assist businesses in deploying new processes, systems, and strategies in order to achieve greater corporate performance. These programs entail developing change initiatives, gaining organizational buy-in, carrying out the initiatives as smoothly as possible, and creating a repeatable model for future success in change activities. Program managers approach change at the program level in a fundamentally different way. They depend on a predetermined, consistent level of performance from the components of the program. For components that are projects, program managers rightfully expect the projects to be delivered on time, on budget, within scope, and with an acceptable level of quality. For other programs and program activities, the program manager should ensure that each be performed in a manner that will contribute positively to the program's outcomes and anticipated benefits, or reduce negative outcomes. For program components, just as in projects, principles of change management are applied to understand and control the variability of each component's schedule, costs, and outcomes. In addition, program managers can create new components or work with the sponsor, other management, or change control board to create or cancel components. This change is made to ensure that benefits are aligned to strategic objectives. Programs use change management in a forward-looking manner to adapt to the evolving environment. This is an iterative process repeated frequently during the performance of a program to ensure it delivers the benefits planned at the start.

▶ **Project change.** In projects, change management is used to help the project manager, team, and stakeholders oversee the amount of variance from the planned specifications (scope and quality), cost, risk, schedule, and other areas of management concern. Agile approaches are led within project life cycles, and change is usually reported in reference to an evolving prototype or release roadmap.

1.9.3 COMPLEXITY

Both programs and projects are associated with complexity. The sources of complexity within programs and projects can be grouped into human behavior, system behavior, and ambiguity (see *Navigating Complexity: A Practice Guide* [14]).

Complexity is an attribute of the environment in which projects and programs exist. It emerges out of the interaction of systems that make up both projects and programs. Programs are made up of projects, components, and other items that are each a system or group of systems that operate together in various ways. Projects are similar, being also made up of systems such as work package teams or technical development staff. The system of systems that make up the program and project landscape may interact simply, in a complicated fashion, or with complexity. The distinguishing factor of complex systems is the lack of, or poor, cause-and-effect relationships between inputs and outputs. Further, a large program may be very complicated with a number of programs and related operations. However, the system of systems that make up the program may have well-defined interfaces and interactions and may be complicated but not complex. The size of the effort or how complicated it is does not drive complexity.

For example, the uncomplex situation just noted may be seen on a new toaster's product delivery and support program. The governing company may have produced a number of very similar products; the technology is well defined; the implementing staff is experienced and organizationally mature; and the stakeholders, including the target buyer, are defined and well known. On the other hand, a project tasked with delivering a new product, say a toaster, may find itself in a complex environment if, for example, the governance structure is not defined and the management and technical teams significantly lack management maturity. In this case, human factors, one of the systems of systems that make up this project, give rise to unpredictable outputs based on ill-defined management inputs. Complexity thus materializes within this project because there is a weak tie between cause-and-effect relationships due to the unpredictability of primarily human behavior as well as nonlinear system behavior. Just as arising complexity in one element of a project may impact the entire project, projects that develop complexity may drive their fostering programs into an environment riddled with complexity.

Projects or programs may develop complexity on an equal basis. The primary difference is the characteristics of the system of systems that make up the project or program and the affected parameters. Table 1-1 shows selected parameters that may act as catalysts for complexity. For example, complexity may arise out of the design of a deliverable. The impact to the project will be directed to the deliverable and may appear through issues with cost, schedule, and project performance. On the other hand, complexity within a specific product development effort may not rise to driving an overall program effort into a complex state, since the larger program management domain may be able to better insulate the overall program system than is possible within the project. This insulation may be inferred, in this case, by realizing that the focus of programs is on benefits creation as opposed to a specific product deliverable. The realization-of-benefits system is at least one layer removed from the project's product development processes or system, and thus may not be affected by complexity associated with this particular product.

Table 1-1 evaluates complexity within projects and programs, discussing various challenges, opportunities, and proactive steps for navigating complexity.

Table 1-1. Comparison of Complexity within Projects and Programs

Parameter	Program	Project
Change Management	Operational and intermediate strategic level • Changing baseline (scope, cost, schedule, and intended benefits) • Changing processes limited to program and project management offices or program and project governance • Changing stakeholders and project personnel • Organization strategic change	Tactical level • Changing baseline (scope, cost, schedule, and intended deliverable) • Changing processes limited to project management office or project governance • Changing stakeholders and project personnel
Benefit Definition (Scope)	Delivery through component elements such as projects and subsidiary programs • Issues may involve integration of multiple project deliveries • Focus is on benefits as opposed to the deliverable	Delivery via developed products or services • Issues tie back to product, service, or capability delivery • Focus is on deliverables
Interdependency	Management between components • Adjusting program baseline (scope, cost, schedule, and intended deliverable) • Creating, monitoring, and controlling components and canceling existing components • Linking tactical product delivery to corporate strategy	Integrated master plan (IMP)/integrated master schedule (IMS) (roadmap-focused management) • Adjusting project baseline (scope, cost, schedule, and intended deliverable) • Creating, monitoring, and controlling work packages; adjusting work packages to deliver requirements
Operational Organization	Close relationship with operations • Ensuring benefits realization through transition and sustainment period with operations	Operations seen as an interface • Project is responsible until the deliverables are provided • Within DevOps, software development transition to operations seen as an interface exercise between development of operations teams
Governance	Mid to senior level • Management has wider view at higher level • Decision options and authority broad and tied more closely to enterprise strategic considerations • Access to key information usually better • Generally better able to handle risks • Link between portfolio (strategic) and project (tactical) governance	Low to mid level • Management focused on project deliveries with a tactical-oriented view • Decision options and authority limited to within the project scope • Information access may be limited as compared to higher levels of management • Governance focused on tactical project concerns
Resources	Required levels of capability and capacity are changing in life cycle • Greater ability to respond to changing resource requirements	Required resources are controlled through program and portfolio actions • In many cases, project must look to higher levels of management to address resource issue
Benefits	Integral result of the program; benefits achieved through delivery and support of capabilities via program components • Benefits realization tied directly to the program outputs	Secondary; results from delivery of quality products, services, and capabilities • Benefits link to product, service, or capability delivery • Incremental delivery and benefits realization may be accomplished via progressive elaboration/rolling wave planning

1.10 PORTFOLIO AND PROGRAM DISTINCTIONS

While portfolios and programs are both collections of projects, activities, and non-project work, there are aspects that clearly differentiate them and help clarify the differences between the two. To clarify the difference between these important organizational constructs, two aspects stand out: relatedness and time.

▶ **Relatedness.** A primary consideration that differentiates programs and portfolios is the concept introduced and implied by the word "related" in the definition of program. In a program, the work included is interdependent, like links in a chain, in that achieving the full intended benefits is dependent on the delivery of all components in the scope of the program. In a portfolio, the work included is related in any way that meets organizational strategic objectives, even if they are not related to one another. Portfolio groupings of work can include efforts staffed from the same resource pool, work delivered to the same client, or work involving the same technology. Other groupings are also valid, such as work performed within the same geographical area or strategic business unit. Work included in the portfolio may span a variety of initiatives, which can be related or independent. The portfolio contains independent activities that the organization may group and manage together for ease of oversight and control.

▶ **Time.** Another attribute that differentiates portfolios from programs is the element of time. Programs may be either ongoing or temporary and include the concept of time as an aspect of the work. Though they may span multiple years or decades, programs are strategic and characterized by the existence of a clearly defined beginning, a future endpoint, and a set of outcomes and planned benefits that are to be achieved during the conduct of the program. Portfolios, on the other hand, while being reviewed on a regular basis for decision-making purposes, are not expected to be constrained to end on a specific date. The various initiatives and work elements defined within the portfolio mostly neither directly relate to one another nor do they rely on one another to achieve benefits. In portfolios, the organization's strategic plan and business cycle dictate the start or end of specific investments, and these investments may serve widely divergent objectives. Additionally, work and investments within the portfolio may continue for years, even decades, or may be altered or terminated by the organization as the business environment changes. Finally, portfolios contain proposals for various initiatives, including operations, programs, and projects that should be evaluated and aligned with the organization's strategic objectives before they are approved. A proposal may exist in the organization's portfolio for an indeterminate length of time, depending on the applicable procedures.

Portfolio management is at a higher level in the organization than program management. Their team competencies are investment-oriented rather than program management-oriented. Portfolio management has strong influence over the programs. It can hold or cancel a program based on its performance and return on investment (compared with other investment opportunities) and the current status of strength of alignment with the organizational strategy.

Table 1-2 highlights the relatedness and time distinctions of portfolio and program management, which enable them to form and carry out schedules to achieve outcomes, objectives, and benefits.

Table 1-2. Relatedness and Time Distinctions of Portfolio and Program Management

	Program	**Portfolio**
Relatedness	**Interdependent** • Program components should be related to achieve the full intended benefits	**Independent** • Portfolio components can be independent
Time	**Temporary endeavor** • Expected to have a defined beginning and future endpoint	**Ongoing** • Not expected to be constrained to end on a specific date • Discrete interval will be defined for the purpose of planning, investment commitment, and monitoring; the cycle will continue with revised goals and objectives

Program Management Principles

In the arena of program management, principles serve as beacons of knowledge, proven practices, and accumulated wisdom. While they serve as foundational guidelines for strategy, decision-making, and problem-solving, principles also represent fundamental norms, truths, or values.

This section includes:

2.1 Stakeholders

2.2 Benefits Realization

2.3 Synergy

2.4 Team of Teams

2.5 Change

2.6 Leadership

2.7 Risk

2.8 Governance

The principles for program management outlined in this publication provide guidance for the behavior of people involved in programs as they influence and shape the program management performance domains (see Section 3) to produce intended benefits. Figure 2-1 demonstrates how the program management principles are positioned above program management performance domains, providing guidance to the activities performed in each performance domain.

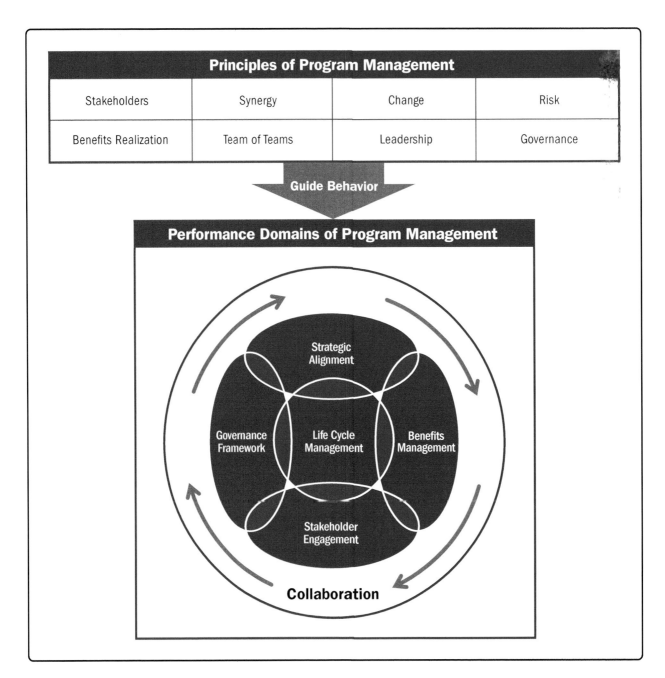

Figure 2-1. Relationship between Program Management Principles and Program Management Performance Domains

Moreover, the principles are broadly based and cover a wide variety of disciplines. Program professionals and stakeholders have abundant opportunities for alignment with the principles and can help influence the way they are implemented and followed during a program's life cycle. The principles of program management can also have areas of overlap with project management and portfolio management principles. Figure 2-2 illustrates this overlap.

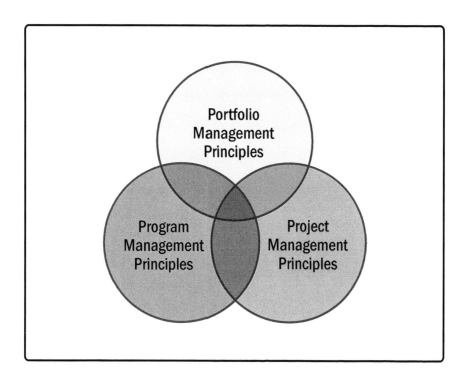

Figure 2-2. Overlap of Portfolio Management, Program Management, and Project Management Principles

An advantage of the principles listed here is that they were formulated and developed by an international community of respected portfolio, program, and project professionals. These accomplished practitioners represent diverse industries, types of projects and programs, and cultural backgrounds, bringing a global view to project and program management.

The principles are listed without any specific weighting or order. The principle statements are described in Sections 2.1 through 2.8. Each section begins with a figure that provides the principle label across the top with the key points described. Following the figure, each principle is further detailed in the text.

The program management principles listed in this standard are:

- ▶ **Stakeholders.** Engage stakeholders at a level commensurate with their impacts or contributions to the program's success (see Section 2.1).

- ▶ **Benefits Realization.** Consistently focus on the program outcomes aligned with organizational strategy (see Section 2.2).

- ▶ **Synergy.** A structured approach that blends portfolio, program, and project management practices to enable the program to accomplish more than what was possible by its individual components (see Section 2.3).

- ▶ **Team of Teams.** Integrate a team structure to create a network of relationships across components to enhance adaptability and resiliency (see Section 2.4).

- ▶ **Change.** Embrace change with an overall focus on program benefits realization (see Section 2.5).

- ▶ **Leadership.** Motivate and unite the program team to keep the program's overall delivery pace and realize expected program benefits (see Section 2.6).

- ▶ **Risk.** Effectively manage program risks to ensure that the program is aligned with the organizational strategy (see Section 2.7).

- ▶ **Governance.** Establish and adopt a proportionate and appropriate program governance framework to control the program as necessary (see Section 2.8).

2.1 STAKEHOLDERS

STAKEHOLDERS

Engage stakeholders proactively to ensure that stakeholder expectations, program benefits, and organizational strategy are all in harmony with one another, and the expected business value of the program is achieved.

▶ Engage stakeholders based on their influence and interests toward the program.

▶ Exploit benefits gained through synergies and mitigate disruptions caused by stakeholder conflicts.

▶ Monitor and act upon stakeholder feedback within the context of the program's life cycle and goals.

Figure 2-3. Principle of Stakeholders

The primary goal of the Stakeholders principle is to ensure that stakeholder expectations, program benefits, and organizational strategy are all in harmony with one another—and the expected business value of the program is achieved and sustained (see Figure 2-3).

This can often be difficult. Program components and benefits realization will be in a continuous state of flux throughout the program's life cycle. To ensure harmony and support strategic alignment compliance and good governance, program managers should continuously analyze the adaptive challenges faced by the program in response to changing stakeholder needs and positions over the program's life cycle. This analysis involves understanding the environment in which the stakeholders exist at that moment, as their needs and positions will be derived from such environmental factors.

Engaging stakeholders is a comprehensive process that should take into consideration stakeholder groups' expectations and influences at the organizational, portfolio, and component levels—with respect to other programs—as well as the external environment in which the program exists.

The program function should determine the level and approach of engagement needed for different stakeholders, including whether they are impacted by the program and their corresponding influences and attitudes toward the success of the program. The program management function should identify, analyze, and proactively engage with stakeholders, and support communications with and among the stakeholders and their respective program component teams.

The Stakeholders principle can be distilled into the following characteristics:

▶ **Proactiveness.** Engages stakeholders by assessing their attitudes and interests toward the program and their change readiness, and motivates them to participate and define the program benefits to ensure strategic alignment with operational strategy and successful delivery of benefits during the program's life cycle.

▶ **Collaboration.** Includes stakeholders in program activities via communications targeted to their needs, interests, requirements, expectations, and wants, according to their change readiness and selected organizational change management strategy speed and scale. A vital part of collaboration involves positively guiding and supporting communications between the stakeholders and the program component teams.

▶ **Monitoring.** Tracks the influences, expectations, needs, feedback, involvement, and attitudes of the program stakeholders throughout the program life cycle.

▶ **Facilitation.** Educates and supports training initiatives as needed within the context of the program or related organizational structure of the program component.

▶ **Adaptivity.** Leverages benefits gained through synergies and mitigating disruptions caused by conflicts. Understands the adaptive challenges faced by the program in response to changing stakeholder needs and positions over the program's life cycle. Determines the changes that need to be made to program components based on the benefits expected by stakeholder groups.

▶ **Clarity.** Gauges the needs of various stakeholder groups, including their roles, interests, influences, and expectations. Evaluates stakeholder attitudes and interests across the organization, including the individual and the external. Ensures that stakeholder expectations, program benefits, and organizational strategy all harmonize with one another.

▶ **Interpersonal skills.** Fosters and builds relationships, takes initiative, and employs integrity and respect. The end goal of leveraging interpersonal skills is to enable everyone to work together to increase the likelihood of program success and, ultimately, customer satisfaction.

2.2 BENEFITS REALIZATION

BENEFITS REALIZATION

Guides those engaged in program management to focus on generating value for the organization by aligning program outcomes with organizational strategy.

▶ Program benefits alignment with organizational strategy takes precedence over the outcome of individual components.

▶ Benefits realized should justify the use of invested resources.

▶ Planned benefits should be agreed upon by key stakeholders and beneficiaries.

▶ Risks should be balanced to support benefits realization.

▶ Governance structures should enable provisioning of adequate resources for benefits realization success.

▶ Program outputs, their outcomes, and the benefits they generate should be transitioned to ongoing operations—including accompanying operational risks, resources, training, and artifacts—and then tracked for sustainment.

Figure 2-4. Principle of Benefits Realization

Benefits realization is the gain realized by one or more organizations and/or groups of people—called beneficiaries—from the outcomes of a program's outputs. Organizations maintain their competitive advantage and fulfill their purpose through ongoing operations and the creation of new products, services, or results, which result in outcomes yielding a variety of benefits to the organization (see Figure 2-4).

It is important to understand that realizing and sustaining benefits is the primary purpose of programs. Furthermore, programs are not just about coordinating the activities of multiple components, but aligning them so the individual outcomes, outputs, or results lead to benefits. A program manager's ultimate responsibility is to ensure that the outputs of their programs create outcomes that generate benefits. This is done through strong program/project team commitment and proper governance.

The Benefits Realization principle creates value for an organization by aligning program outcomes with organizational strategy. Depending on the type, nature, and context of a program, benefits may be realized as soon as specific outcomes are produced, or may require the integration of a number of outcomes before they can be realized.

A program achieves benefits realization through alignment of internal activities with external drivers. Alignment is required across the components within the program, with other programs, and with an overlying portfolio to which the program may belong. Most crucially, alignment is required with the organization's strategy. The program achieves benefits realization by closing gaps between the expected outcomes to ensure strategic alignment.

The difference between realized benefits and the delivery costs of a program is a program's added value, which is represented through a combination of quantitative and qualitative factors. Although it is arguable that some intangible benefits cannot be measured quantitatively, organizations need to assign a value to such benefits to justify and manage spending and investment. Organizations may attempt to measure the realization of these intangible benefits through the use of questionnaires and surveys.

The outputs of some programs may create outcomes that start to generate benefits for beneficiaries as soon as the output is created or shortly thereafter. Other program benefits realization may occur immediately after integration of the program outputs, while in other cases, benefits may be realized long after the program is concluded and the program team disbanded. Benefits are realized incrementally throughout the program or after the program ends.

Program outputs, their outcomes, and the benefits they generate should be transitioned to ongoing operations—including accompanying operational risks, resources, training, and artifacts—and then tracked for sustainment. Transition work is part of the scope of the program. Without proper and effective benefits realization management, programs may achieve their outcomes but fail to accomplish strategic goals.

The benefits resulting from the outcomes of a program across its entire life cycle should justify the use of the resources invested in the program. Normally, these benefits are proactively planned and provide the basis for organizational sponsorship of the program. However, the benefits realization management mindset and methodologies should be adaptive. This approach may result in terminating or modifying components that will not result in benefits, or initiating new, unplanned components in the interest of overall benefits realization.

A program should only be initiated after strategic justification is completed and agreed upon. Anticipated benefits should be unambiguously articulated and quantified to all stakeholders and beneficiaries. This action is important because proactively planning and tracking benefits guides analysis and decision-making throughout the management of the program. During the program's life cycle, outputs and their outcomes need to be managed, and sometimes integrated, to realize overall benefits.

Planned benefits should be agreed upon by key stakeholders and the appropriate beneficiaries. Most benefits are identified at a high level early in the program and then progressively elaborated throughout the program life cycle. These benefits should be analyzed, captured, and communicated by means of the program artifacts (e.g., business cases, benefits realization plans, the program/component charters, program management plans, program roadmap). These artifacts should then be evaluated and updated as part of program management. Additionally, any benefits realization artifacts should be periodically verified for alignment with organizational strategy. This alignment with organizational strategy will enable the program and the organization to effectively track progress toward achieving planned benefits.

Benefits realization changes the focus of program risk management from control to balance. Benefits realization requires balancing risk across the program to achieve the program's overall benefits, but not necessarily reduce the threat to individual program components.

The success of benefits realization requires proper governance and allocation of adequate resources. Benefits realization management requires adequately provisioned resources, working within a clear governance structure, with those responsible for managing and achieving the agreed and anticipated benefits being identified correctly as accountable and authorized to do so. This governance structure also requires and ensures the proper transition of outputs, their outcomes, and resultant benefits from a program into operations, as well as accompanying risks, resources, training, and artifacts.

Benefits realization culminates in the sustainment of benefits during or after the program's life cycle. It is within the program's scope to create the enablers (processes, measurements, metrics, tools) that result in the achievement and tracking of sustainment during ongoing operations and post-program closure.

2.3 SYNERGY

SYNERGY

The continual evaluation and navigation of component complexities and dependencies for optimization across the program, creating more than what was achievable by its individual component parts.

▶ Use a structured or agile approach that blends project and program management good practices to enable the program to accomplish more than what was possible by its individual components.

▶ Drive changes to individual components in a manner that optimizes the whole of the program, including the creation of new components, cancellation of components, and changes to components midlife.

▶ Foster the right conditions and ensure the proper culture is in place for projects and programs to be synergistic.

▶ Continually evaluate and navigate component complexities for optimization across the program.

▶ Align the program components with the program management plan, capacity, capabilities, and performance domain efforts in order to optimize the realization of objectives.

Figure 2-5. Principle of Synergy

Synergy is a known beneficial concept, but achieving It takes leadership and management skills to optimize across projects, programs, and the portfolio, as well as the totality of principles and domains across the enterprise. The core concept is to unite efforts and create an aligned program component structure and requirements, thereby optimizing benefits by balancing effectiveness and efficiency. Synergy efforts should align with beneficiaries and program strategy as well as enhance program benefits realization (see Figure 2-5).

The Synergy principle drives predictive, adaptive, or hybrid approaches to inform project and program management performance domains to enable the program to achieve more than what was achievable by its individual program components. Such achievement may be in respect to the effectiveness, efficiency, payback period, or other elements pertinent to the achievement of the strategic objectives the program should fulfill. The Synergy principle should drive changes to individual components to ensure alignment across components in a manner that optimizes the whole of the program, including but not limited to the creation of new components, cancellation of components, and changes to components midlife. Synergy can foster the right conditions and ensure enablers are in place (at both the organizational and program levels) for a culture that allows all program management principles and performance domains to be synergistic.

According to *A Guide to the Project Management Body of Knowledge* (*PMBOK® Guide*) [1], projects are defined as "temporary endeavors undertaken to create a unique product, service, or result." Programs, meanwhile, are defined as "related projects, subsidiary programs, and program activities managed in a coordinated manner to obtain benefits not available from managing them individually." Programs are designed to unite the related efforts to create more benefits than the sum of the program component parts or enhance control over them. Program teams can create, manage, and maintain an integrated schedule of components, if not accomplished at the portfolio level, to structure program components from initiation to strategic objective realization.

In program management, synergies may be proactively sought, or reactively arise, within one or more components across principles and domains at the portfolio, program, and project levels. Several principles and domains that cross the portfolio, program, and project structure, including Stakeholder Engagement, Risk (uncertainties), Strategic Alignment, and Life Cycle Management, can be strengthened by the principle of Synergy. Outcomes at the project level, benefits at the program level, and value at the portfolio level can be further enhanced with the Synergy principle, especially when a portfolio's unique capacity and capability domains are also considered at the program level when applying the Synergy principle. This can be critical when a program is not within a portfolio management structure.

The demonstration of synergy across and within capabilities and capacities could include the development of a capability that is shared across multiple program components, and that may have not previously existed within the organization. This shared capability may, in turn, lead to increased capacity, cost reductions, improved quality, greater compliance, and the development of reusable capabilities. These efforts can be performed at the portfolio or program levels, where governance from a portfolio is limited or domain performance is delegated to the program.

The application of the Synergy principle regarding strategy and benefits could be the uniting of related benefits that align with one or more strategic objectives cutting across projects and other components of programs or portfolios. The synergy might be the commonalities in delivering these benefits in a more resource-efficient manner (at a reduced cost, staffing, or timeline) by centralizing efforts for improved performance, enhancing control over the components, or creating interim value necessary for the realization of the strategic objective that the program is trying to achieve. Likewise, synergy may also be reactive, rather than proactive, where the delivery or attainment of certain benefits results in a new strategic (competitive) advantage or goal not previously envisioned or proactively planned.

The manifestation of synergy in the areas of risk or complexity could be the ability to better address negative risks or uncertainties or capitalize on opportunities yielded from complex structures and relationships (e.g., between program components, resources, people, or situations external or internal to the program). Risk, or the manifestation thereof, may also result in the loss of synergy and its effects on the program, either temporarily or permanently.

The benefits of synergy to stakeholders can include improved collaboration, interaction, cooperation, and communication, which may yield advantages such as the discovery of strategic commonalities or the reduction of communication overheads and situational complexities.

It is important to note that synergy can, and should, occur among the components of the program at the component level, but may also occur between an element of one component and an element of another component.

2.4 TEAM OF TEAMS

TEAM OF TEAMS

Team of teams is a characterization of an integrated team structure that creates a network relationship across products and processes.

A network of teams that is connected vertically and horizontally forms a structure that allows for a union of shared strategy and empowered execution that enables adaptability and resiliency in the face of complexity and uncertainty.

▶ Utilize the appropriate leadership styles, techniques, and networking tools to effectively and efficiently manage the program and its components.

▶ Team leaders, whether appointed by senior managers or executives or selected by team members, should exhibit leadership principles within the team of teams framework.

▶ The team's size should stay within a reasonable boundary.

Figure 2-6. Principle of Team of Teams

The Team of Teams principle characterizes an integrated team structure that creates a network of relationships across products and processes. This network is connected vertically and horizontally, forming a structure that allows for shared strategy and empowered execution. The result: adaptability and resiliency in the face of complexity and uncertainty (see Figure 2-6).

Team structure is a key aspect of the organizational governance system, which itself is key to value delivery. At the project level, the Team of Teams principle cultivates a collaborative project team environment. The fundamentals of a team of teams—such as agreements, structure, processes, and more, as outlined at the project level—also apply to the program or portfolio levels. The Team of Teams principle also addresses activities and functions associated with those individuals who are responsible for producing project deliverables that affect business outcomes. More information can be found in the PMI publication *Choose Your WoW! A Disciplined Agile Approach to Optimizing Your Way of Working* [15].

The program manager leads the team of teams responsible for achieving program objectives. They ensure the overall program structure and applied program management process enable the program and its component teams to successfully complete the work and deliver anticipated benefits.

As indicated earlier in this section, the team of teams should design an integrated team structure that builds a network of relationships spanning the product and process activities and deliverables. This network of teams, which can be connected vertically and horizontally, allows for shared strategy, more effective execution of tasks, and greater adaptability and resiliency—even in the most complex, uncertain times. Such enhanced flexibility enables a shifting of focus and adaptable reconfiguration of the team's network as the program's component activities evolve.

A program's team of teams structure should have a strategy to achieve through defined and undefined forums for communication, enhanced transparency, and empowered execution. These actions provide clear leadership and managerial authority through defined boundaries within the program and component work breakdown structure (WBS), including team-dynamic-management methods such as a responsibility assignment matrix (RAM) and a responsible, accountable, consulted, and informed (RACI) matrix.

A program management information system is a critical tool for the success of a wholly integrated team structure, and the organizational culture should allow the program team to use it properly. In complex efforts, such as programs, doing the right work to focus on effectiveness is also critical, as well as doing the right work to focus on efficiency. The Team of Teams principle will need to balance effectiveness and efficiency in determining the structure.

Managing a program's team of teams is complex. Much of what a leader needs to consider in forming teams is evolving and depends on the culture of the organization.

2.5 CHANGE

CHANGE

Manage program change to improve effectiveness and efficiency of benefits realization, delivery, and sustainment during the program life cycle and after its transition to an organization's operations.

▶ Use a structured approach to change to help the program management team, the program, and its components respond to internal and/or external factors that may impact the program's ability to deliver, realize, integrate, or transition program benefits.

▶ Change can originate from internal influences or external sources.

▶ Change adoption requires fostering the right conditions and culture across the program and its components.

▶ Change should be results-oriented and evaluated against the program's strategic goals and benefits to be realized.

▶ Enablers of successful change management include assessment, adoption and assimilation, motivation, engagement and communication, urgency and speed, and embracing risk.

Figure 2-7. Principle of Change

Managing program change effectively is critical to improving the efficiency of benefits realization, delivery, and sustainment during a program's life cycle and after its transition to an organization's operations (see Figure 2-7).

Given the progressively elaborative nature of programs—and the span of time in which they may exist—it is inevitable that there will be a significant amount of change to program structure, components, the program management plan, and so forth. The ultimate motivation behind such change should be to ensure the program meets its objectives and delivers the anticipated benefits as measured by the effectiveness and efficiency metrics defined by the program.

Change can originate from internal or external sources and influences. Internal sources can involve the need for a new capability or synergy, the response to a performance gap, a transformation, or a change in capacity. External sources may include technological advances, demographic changes, compliance needs, or socioeconomic pressures. Furthermore, internal change also refers to shifts within the program, while external change refers to the need to adapt the organization to exploit the benefits created by the program. Change can also arise from identified risks or opportunities. For programs that contain components that cater to paying customers (business projects), then change can also be due to responding to changes in the market or customer demands. Change adoption requires fostering the right conditions and culture across the program and its components, as well as across the performing organization.

Programs need to align the change management process with the program life cycle and mobilize stakeholders and resources across program components. Programs accept and adapt to change to optimize the delivery of benefits as the program's components deliver outcomes.

Projects, meanwhile, focus on keeping change managed and controlled, whereas portfolios continuously monitor change in the broader internal and external environments and embrace change with an overall focus on value. Enterprise project management offices (EPMOs) facilitate organizational change management at all levels, including program-level change management. In contrast, portfolios have an organizational horizon of change management that varies with the strategic objectives of the organization, rather than a focus on any specific program by itself. Change at the portfolio level may modify the program, leading to the cancellation of the program or the initiation of new programs.

Managing change at the program level requires component-transition change management throughout all stages of a program's life cycle, from definition to delivery to closure. This change management includes the ability to alter the direction of a component, including adding, canceling, or terminating components to the program. Change management at the component level is tactical, to affect deliverables, whereas change management at the program level is strategic and affects the delivery of intended benefits. Change management factors include:

▶ **Definition.** Identify the need for change in the program, assess readiness for change, and define the change approach.

▶ **Analysis.** Evaluate the impact of the change at both the program and component levels.

▶ **Delivery.** Make decisions related to components and mobilize resources.

▶ **Closure.** Ensure that all program artifacts are updated to effect any changes.

Programs proactively use change management to keep components and intended benefits aligned with changes in organizational strategy and in the environment in which they are performed. Program change management identifies sources of change, such as the volatility of the enterprise environmental factors (EEFs), the sensitivity of the proposed program's business case, changes in organizational strategy, and the frequency and magnitude of changes that may arise from components during program delivery. The program then evaluates the impact of these changes and proposes actions to accommodate them. Thus, programs foster a culture that embraces change and risk, rather than controlling the nature of change and risk. This approach allows programs to navigate complexities brought about through change in order to enable successful outcomes.

2.6 LEADERSHIP

LEADERSHIP

Inspire, unite, and lead the program team to align the program vision with the team's efforts and delivery throughout the program life cycle to realize the desired benefits, value, and outcomes.

▶ Show empathy for the perspectives of both the program team and other stakeholders.

▶ Create a climate of trust and consistency for the whole program team.

▶ Facilitate negotiations and resolve conflicts within the program team and between the team and other stakeholders.

▶ Ensure consistency in the program's vertical support and horizontal coordination.

▶ Empower each component manager with the authority and autonomy to lead their projects within program governance limitations.

▶ Coach and mentor fellow program team members. Adapt the leadership style to the situation and gain a keen understanding of political savvy within the program and organization.

Figure 2-8. Principle of Leadership

Program leadership motivates and unites the program team, harnessing its energy, enthusiasm, and vision to maintain the delivery pace of benefits and align with program strategy—throughout the entire program life cycle (see Figure 2-8).

Program leadership complements program management throughout the program life cycle, and is more than just getting things done. It is about sharing and agreeing on a compelling, strategically aligned view of the future, connecting with the program stakeholders, and engaging them in the temporary work while delivering and realizing program benefits together.

The program manager establishes and maintains the timely, appropriate pace of program delivery in order to enable the organization to successfully achieve the expected program benefits with strategic alignment. Program leadership includes leading a program team, engaging senior leadership, integrating program work, connecting cross-functional interdependencies, proactively identifying risks, and fully realizing program benefits.

Program managers focus on establishing and executing the mechanisms that empower decision-making and work within specific delegated limits of authority in program governance. Program governance creates both the governance structure and practices to guide the program. Program governance can also provide executive leadership, oversight, and control. The program manager performs a very important leadership role in this, establishing consistency in the program's vertical support and horizontal coordination.

With an increasingly complicated context for program leadership, program managers should build effective leadership in program teams that can differ geographically, culturally, organizationally, and across time zones. Effective program infrastructure (such as a videoconferencing system for a global program team) enables a program manager to focus on leading the program team in the realization of the identified benefits. It is important to empower component managers with the autonomy to lead their project teams. Authorized autonomy in program governance requires efficient and effective program leadership. Such effectiveness reflects the strength of governance execution, and the less the program manager intervenes in the component projects, the better the leadership effect and the higher the component project teams' morale.

To influence the program environment, the program manager needs a level of emotional, social, and cognitive intelligence to be aware of the program team's dynamics. Emotional intelligence refers to our ability to identify our own and others' emotions; motivate ourselves to improve; and use our emotional capability to guide our thoughts, inspire enthusiasm, and show a willingness to shoulder responsibility. Emotional intelligence, for both the program manager and the whole program team, is critical to the program's success. The leader's positive self-awareness has a layered diffusion effect and distributes this healthy energy throughout the entire program, reaching team members' high levels of commitment and motivation. This is critical because the wisdom, skill, passion, and experience of each individual team member are essential for success.

Program managers should be self-aware enough to know they cannot personally achieve any of the outcomes for which they are striving without the impact and influence of other people. Leading with values makes the program manager more authentic as a leader and helps to create a climate of trust and consistency for the whole program team. Without trust in the program team, the program manager is unable to delegate work to component managers or give them the autonomy to deliver the program's component projects effectively and efficiently. Trust is the foundation of effective collaboration in program management. There are three kinds of trust: personality-based trust, cognitive-based trust, and institutional-based trust. Consistency is equally important and should permeate all decision-making, metrics, evaluation of performance, and other management processes. The leadership style for program management depends partly on the situation and focuses on managing relationships and resolving conflicts to boost team morale and realize program benefits.

A program manager should perceive and build relationships as the route to performance and devote sufficient time and focus to the program team members and working climate. Engaging others' hearts and minds is key to making sure people feel like they are integral parts of the program team. A leadership style that shares the wide purpose of the work and allows people to do their best and develop mastery will motivate them further and create an environment in which the team and its individuals can develop and thrive.

To lead the whole program team to success, the program manager should have these seven interpersonal and personal skills:

▶ **Empathy.** This is the ability of program managers to experience others' feelings and be sensitive to their needs. Empathy involves perceiving the emotions of others, dealing with others' perspectives, celebrating their successes, establishing harmonious interpersonal relationships, and working in harmony with various program stakeholders.

▶ **Respect.** The program manager should be able to treat others with consideration, to value what they bring to the program, to appreciate their skills and the work they do, and to promptly acknowledge and appreciate them.

▶ **Courage.** Courage implies there is a challenge to be pushed through and a fear that needs to be overcome. The program manager needs bravery to lead a team of diverse individuals to conquer a challenge by trying new things and finding new ways of working. By tapping into such courage, the program manager will be encouraged to confront uncertainty, challenge the status quo, and find a new way forward. Courage is contagious and instills a positive energy within the whole program team.

▶ **Political savvy.** The program manager should understand that politics is a behavioral aspect of program management that should be managed to attain program success. Program managers should be politically sensible by showing sensitivity to the interests of the most powerful and influential program stakeholders and demonstrating good judgment by acting with integrity. It is important that a program manager possesses both a keen understanding of the organization and the political savvy necessary to build strong relationships to leverage and influence the key program stakeholders effectively.

▶ **Collaboration.** It is vital for program managers to work with component managers to break down silos and encourage openness of participation within the team, negotiate and resolve conflict within and among the program team and other stakeholders, and generate consensus on the way forward to overcome obstacles to program progress.

▶ **Facilitation.** Program managers need good facilitation skills to help multiple program stakeholders, such as component managers, to communicate and collaborate effectively. Core facilitation skills include the ability to draw out varying opinions and viewpoints among team members to create discussion and collaboration boundaries, and to summarize and synthesize details into useful information and strategy.

▶ **Influence.** The influencing traits of successful program managers include being socially adept at interacting with others, assessing all aspects of information and behavior without passing judgment or injecting bias, and effectively communicating their point of view to change an opinion or alter a course of action. Program managers need to be able to influence decisions and motivate a program team through effective communication, unite the program team and have them work together, and sustain the overall delivery pace for the program.

Program leadership complements program management. The program manager uses strong leadership to ensure program governance effectiveness and maintain the right pace for delivering and realizing program benefits. With the aforementioned seven traits, program managers can strengthen relationships and resolve conflicts to motivate component managers to lead their teams well.

2.7 RISK

RISK	
Proactively manage program risks throughout the program life cycle to achieve benefits that are aligned with strategic objectives and build risk response plans across the different program components.	▶ Ensure the program risk threshold is aligned with the organization's risk appetite. ▶ Identify and evaluate risks throughout the program life cycle. ▶ Implement the practical use of benchmarking. ▶ Effectively manage the component dependencies of the program. ▶ Address risks related to business viability throughout the program continuously.

Figure 2-9. Principle of Risk

A risk is an uncertain event or condition that, if it occurs, has a positive or negative effect on one or more program objectives. Risks can have both positive and negative impacts on programs. Negative risks, often referred to as threats, affect the implementation of programs and realization of benefits. Positive risks, usually referred to as opportunities, help foster effective, efficient program implementation and increased realization of benefits (see Figure 2-9).

Programs are inherently complex in nature, due to groups of related components and their interactions with one another. Program complexity includes technical and sociopolitical factors, schedule and cost constraints, and the broader environment in which the program is managed.

Consequently, it is vital to proactively manage program risks throughout the program life cycle in order to achieve benefits that are aligned with strategic objectives and build and implement risk response plans across diverse program components.

Programs are executed to achieve benefits and organizational strategic objectives. An effective risk management strategy is essential to ensuring a program aligns with the broader organizational strategy. Thus, program risk thresholds should consider organizational risk appetite, which is an assessment of an organization's willingness to accept and deal with risks.

Risk identification and analysis is an ongoing effort throughout the program life cycle. This process should address two main factors:

▶ Risks that may be encountered during the life cycle of the program and their impact on achieving the program objectives within traditional time and cost perspectives; and

▶ Risks that may affect the realization of benefits during program implementation and after program transition.

During risk identification and analysis, it is important to guard against optimistic bias, which is a subset of rational correctness. This bias is the tendency to forecast future events in an optimistic or positive way. In program planning, this bias neglects to identify and evaluate risks in a structured way. Planners should recognize that most projects experience delays and cost overruns are common. Optimistic biases can be lessened by benchmarking against risks observed in other programs. This will help identify planned versus actual variances observed in prior programs and will provide realistic expectations.

For a program to be successful, it is crucial to manage its respective risks, their interdependencies within program components, and their impact on overall achievement of program benefits. The program roadmap helps identify the program component interactions, and further program interface and integration reveal significant touchpoints. An early focus on dependencies and the interfaces among components and their respective complexities is critical for program success. Risk assessment should address both human behavior and system behavior when considering complexities in programs and should align dependencies accordingly.

Programs are created to achieve benefits. Addressing risks early is necessary and proactive, keeping in mind that uncertainties always exist and will always appear during the program. Organizational risk appetite will guide the program governance approach to managing risk to achieve business viability. This risk management approach can be accomplished by managing strategic risk representation during the program and setting expectations by rebaselining the program approach and benefits achievement.

Program benefits realization is not limited to program implementation, meaning that program risk management activities should transfer identified risks—along with supporting analysis and response information—to the appropriate organizational risk register. This task may be managed by a different organizational group, such as an EPMO or organizational program management office, rather than the one intended to realize the benefits.

2.8 GOVERNANCE

GOVERNANCE

Program governance ensures the program is managed appropriately.

▶ Enable transparency, responsibility, accountability, sustainability, and fairness.

▶ Align with policy, oversight, control, integration, and decision-making.

▶ Adhere to the governance practice of the organization and portfolio.

▶ Manage issues and risks to support decision-making.

▶ Oversee changes in the progress of program components in order to eliminate arbitrariness and establish standardized project management practice across the organization.

▶ Governance should be right-sized for the needs of the program.

Figure 2-10. Principle of Governance

Program governance comprises the framework, functions, processes, and tools by which a program is monitored, managed, and supported in order to meet organizational strategic and operational goals. A key aspect of governance is establishing a framework within which the lines of authority are clear, the responsibility and accountability of each position defined, and the levels of decision-making structured to enable effective and efficient delivery of the program and its components (see Figure 2-10).

The focus of program governance is the delivery of program benefits by establishing the systems and methods by which a program and its strategy are defined, authorized, monitored, and supported by its sponsoring organization. A program governance framework, when well designed, provides practices for effective decision-making while also managing change within the progress of program components.

The Governance principle can be distilled into the following characteristics:

▶ **Transparency.** Enabling relevant access to program information while maintaining responsibility, accountability, sustainability, and fairness across all program elements—and providing a platform or voice for concerns.

▶ **Oversight.** Retaining oversight on policy, control, integration, and decision-making as it pertains to the program, while guiding and promoting desirable behaviors to ensure success and desired outcomes.

▶ **Compliance.** Creating a framework to ensure the program is managed appropriately, following the governance practice of the organization, and adhering to regulations or frameworks with which all programs should comply.

▶ **Resiliency.** Managing risk; overseeing impacts, issues, and risks that support decision-making; and maintaining organizational resiliency as a governance function.

▶ **Adaptivity.** Managing changes at the strategic level and overseeing changes in the progress of program components within the standardized project management practice that exists in the organization and in the governance framework.

Governance occurs across all phases of a program's life cycle. A proposed program will be presented to the governance team for approval, funding, and authorization. During the program-strategy-alignment process, which is initiated and runs until the end of the program life cycle, the management processes to identify and quantify environmental factors, outcomes, and benefits—and to identify and manage program risks—should be executed and controlled within the program governance framework, if possible.

Program governance can be performed through the actions of a review and decision-making group charged with endorsing or approving recommendations regarding a program under its authority. In keeping with the principle of "most programs, most of the time," however, most programs will have to deal with multiple governance bodies, not just one through which all governance functions are performed.

The program manager is responsible for overseeing or coordinating the governance systems or bodies while managing the program's daily activities. Program managers should also collaborate with governance bodies to ensure the program's continued alignment with an organizational strategy. The program manager should make sure the program team understands and abides by the governance procedures and underlying governance principles.

The concept of governance should not only be concerned with the top-line oversight of a program. When issues or concerns escalate, they often fall under the individuals overseeing and monitoring the governance framework, processes, and implementation, including the program manager. Thus, governance should also seek to be a platform or voice for important, escalating, or high-priority issues. These concerns could include anything from social issues to workplace cultural norms that may have an impact on the organization or, in this case, the program.

Program Management Performance Domains

Program management performance domains are complementary groupings of related areas of activity or function that uniquely characterize and differentiate the activities of one performance domain from others, within the full scope of program management work.

This section includes:

3.1 Program Management Performance Domain Definitions

3.2 Program Management Performance Domain Interactions

3.3 Strategic Alignment

3.4 Benefits Management

3.5 Stakeholder Engagement

3.6 Governance Framework

3.7 Collaboration

3.8 Life Cycle Management

Program managers actively carry out work within multiple program management performance domains during all program management phases. The interactions among program management performance domains, which are optimized through Collaboration (see Section 3.7), are shown in Figure 3-1.

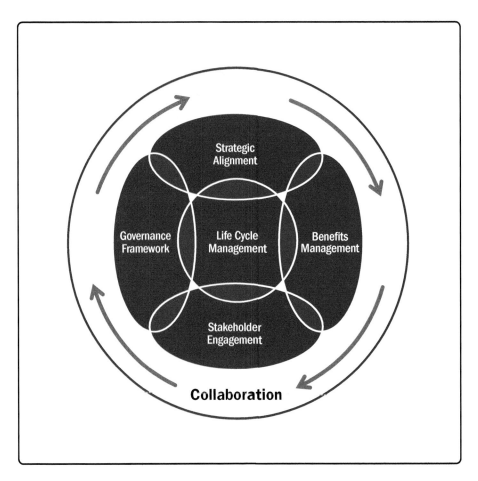

Figure 3-1. Program Management Performance Domains

The Standard for Program Management

3.1 PROGRAM MANAGEMENT PERFORMANCE DOMAIN DEFINITIONS

Organizations launch programs to deliver benefits and achieve agreed-upon outcomes affecting their operations. Programs are related projects, subsidiary programs, and program activities managed in a coordinated manner to obtain benefits not available from managing them individually. Program objectives are achieved through the actions, guidance, and leadership of the program manager, who works to implement program management principles within the context of the six program management performance domains. Together, these principles and performance domains are critical to the success of the program. The program management performance domains are:

▶ **Strategic Alignment.** Identifies program outputs and outcomes to provide benefits aligned with organizational strategy goals and objectives.

▶ **Benefits Management.** Defines, creates, optimizes, delivers, and sustains the benefits provided by the program.

▶ **Stakeholder Engagement.** Identifies and analyzes stakeholder needs and manages expectations and communications to foster stakeholder support.

▶ **Governance Framework.** Enables and performs program decision-making, establishes practices to support the program, maintains program oversight, and ensures compliance with standards and regulations.

▶ **Collaboration.** Creates and maintains synergy across stakeholders, both internal and external, to optimize benefits delivery and realization.

▶ **Life Cycle Management.** Manages the program life cycle and the phases required to facilitate program definition, delivery, and closure.

These performance domains run concurrently throughout the duration of the program. It is within these domains that the program manager and the program team perform their activities. Every program requires some activity in each of these performance domains during the entire program life cycle (see Section 3.8); the nature and complexity of the program being implemented determine the degree of activity required within a particular domain at any point in time. Work within these domains is iterative in nature and repeated frequently. Each domain is described in detail in its respective section within this standard.

3.2 PROGRAM MANAGEMENT PERFORMANCE DOMAIN INTERACTIONS

As depicted in Figure 3-1, all program management performance domains interact with one another throughout the course of the program and should be optimized through effective and efficient collaboration (see Section 3.7). When organizations pursue similar programs, however, the interactions among the performance domains can be similar and often repetitive. All six domains interact with one another with varying degrees of intensity. These are the areas in which program managers will spend their time while implementing the program. The domains reflect the higher-level organizational functions that are essential aspects of the program manager's role, regardless of the size of the organization, industry or business focus, or geographic location.

Performance domains across portfolios, programs, and projects are related and also interact with one another. As noted, when projects are not governed under a program/portfolio, or when programs are not governed by a portfolio, program and project managers should consider the broad set of domain functions for applicability to their leadership and management challenges.

3.3 STRATEGIC ALIGNMENT

Strategic Alignment is the program management performance domain that identifies program outputs and outcomes to provide benefits aligned with the organization's strategic goals and objectives.

This section includes:

3.3.1 Program Business Case

3.3.2 Program Charter

3.3.3 Program Management Plan

3.3.4 Environmental Assessments

3.3.5 Program Risk Management Strategy

3.3.6 Interactions with Program Management Principles and Other Program Management Performance Domains

Programs are designed to align with organizational strategy and facilitate the realization of organizational benefits. To accomplish this, program managers should have a thorough understanding of how the program will fulfill the portfolio and organizational strategy, goals, and objectives, as well as possess the skills needed to match the program with the organization's long-term vision.

When an organization develops its strategy, there is typically an initial evaluation and selection process, which could be formal or informal, to help determine which initiatives to approve, reject, or defer as part of the organization's portfolio management practice.

The more mature an organization is in terms of program and project management, the more likely it will have a formalized process for program selection such as a portfolio review board or steering committee. An appropriate decision-making body will sign a program charter defining the strategic objectives and benefits a particular program is expected to deliver. The program charter is a document signed by a sponsor that authorizes the program management team to use organizational resources to execute the program, and it links the program to the organization's strategic objectives. It also plans the scope and purpose of a proposed program presented to the individual or group tasked with governance to obtain approval, funding, and authorization. The program charter confirms the commitment of organizational resources, triggering the program planning phase.

While project managers lead and direct the work on their projects, it is the program manager's responsibility to provide alignment of individual project management plans with the program's goals and intended benefits to promote synergy in achieving the organization's strategic goals and objectives. Figure 3-2 depicts the components of Strategic Alignment.

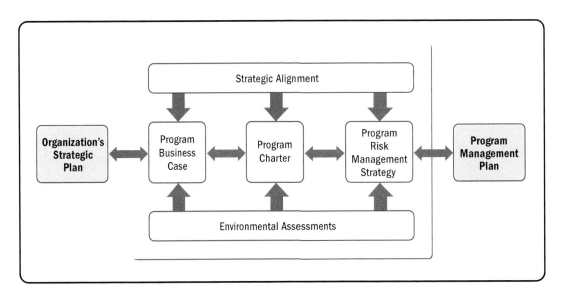

Figure 3-2. Elements of Strategic Alignment

Strategic Alignment is initiated with the development of a program business case. The documented cost-benefit analysis is used to establish the validity of the benefits to be delivered by a program. Beyond monetary, benefits may include such things as tools, new approaches, expanding approved suppliers, and other items. Program business cases may include an analysis justifying the need for a program by defining how that program's expected outcomes would support the organization's strategic goals and objectives. In addition to establishing the validity of potential program benefits, the program business case serves as an input to the program charter and, subsequently, the program management plan. These three documents are established as part of program formulation activities (see Section 3.8.1.1).

During the execution of the program formulation subphase, the strategic alignment process is initiated and runs until the end of the program life cycle. During this time, the management processes to identify and quantify environmental factors, outcomes, and benefits—and to identify and manage program risks—are executed and controlled within the governance framework. When misalignment is identified, the program management plan or organization's strategic goals and objectives should be revised to ensure alignment. This activity may occur in research, where the results of a program determine that a given line of research is not likely to succeed, and the organization then changes its strategy—sometimes without canceling or discontinuing the program—to better leverage the results.

3.3.1 PROGRAM BUSINESS CASE

Organizations build strategy to define how their vision should be achieved. The completion of the strategic planning cycle results in the creation or update of the organization's strategic goals and objectives, which are then documented in the organization's strategic plan. The organization's vision and mission are used as inputs to the strategic planning cycle and are reflected throughout the strategic plan. The organization's strategic plan is subdivided into a set of organizational initiatives that are influenced in part by market dynamics, customer and partner requests, shareholders, government regulations, the organization's strengths and weaknesses, risk exposure, and competitor plans and actions. These initiatives may be grouped into portfolios to be executed during a predetermined period.

Programs are formally evaluated, selected, and authorized based on their alignment with, and support of, the organization's strategic plan, usually as part of its governance practices. To facilitate alignment and goal setting, the organization's strategic plan is further delineated as a set of goals and objectives that may have measurable elements such as products, deliverables, benefits, cost, and timing, among others. The goal of linking the program to the organization's strategic plan is to design and manage a program that will help the organization achieve its strategic goals and objectives, and to balance its use of resources while optimizing value. This optimization is achieved through the program business case. During program definition, the program manager collaborates with key sponsors and stakeholders to develop the business case, which assesses the program's investment against the intended benefits. The business case can be basic and high level or detailed and comprehensive. It usually describes key parameters that may be used to assess the objectives and constraints for the intended program.

The business case may include details about the program outcomes, approved concepts, issues, high-level risks and opportunity assessments, key assumptions, business and operational impacts, cost-benefit analysis, alternative solutions, financial analysis, intrinsic and extrinsic benefits, market demands or barriers, potential profits, social needs, environmental influences, legal implications, time to market, constraints, and the extent to which the program aligns with the organization's strategic plan. The business case describes the intent and authority behind the drivers of the program and the underlying philosophy of the business need. It serves as both approval and justification for the investment that will be expended to deliver the program benefits in line with the organization's strategy.

The business case is required as one of the document deliverables before the program can be chartered and may be considered as the primary justification document for an investment decision. It also describes success criteria to be maintained throughout the program. The variance between the achieved and the planned outcomes is calculated to measure the success of the program.

One such measurement of success determined in a business case involves intangible (or nontangible) benefits. These are benefits that a program intends to produce but may not be measured in units of money; examples include brand awareness, regulatory compliance, or enhanced customer experience. Organizations should strive to monitor these intangibles. (For more information about benefits management, see Section 3.4.)

The business case, once approved, indicates the investment earmarked for achieving a component of the organization's strategic objectives. Any expenditure outside of the approved business case is a deviation from the strategy and represents misalignment. It is the role of the Governance Framework performance domain (see Section 3.6) to ensure such deviation does not occur.

3.3.2 PROGRAM CHARTER

Following approval of the business case, the program steering committee or designated body (see Section 3.6.2.2) authorizes the program management team by means of the program charter. Derived from the business case, the program charter is a document that assigns and authorizes a program manager and defines the scope and purpose of a proposed program presented to the governance authority to obtain approval, funding, and authorization.

Key elements of a program charter consist of the program scope, assumptions, constraints, high-level risks, high-level benefits and their realization, goals and objectives, success criteria, timing, key stakeholders, outcomes, resource allocation, and other provisions that tie the program to the business case, thereby enabling strategic alignment. The contents of the program charter generally consist of the following:

- ▶ **Justification.** Why is the program important and what does it achieve?
- ▶ **Vision.** What is the end state and how will it benefit the organization?

- ▶ **Strategic alignment.** What are the key strategic drivers and the program's relationship to the organizational strategic objectives and any other ongoing strategic initiatives?

- ▶ **Scope.** What is included within the program and what is considered out of scope at a high level?

- ▶ **Benefits.** What are the key intended gains to be realized to achieve the program's vision and benefits?

- ▶ **Benefit strategy.** What is the approach to ensure the realization of the planned benefits? (See Section 3.4 for more information on benefits management.)

- ▶ **Assumptions and constraints.** What are the assumptions, constraints, dependencies, and external factors, and how have they shaped or limited the program's objectives?

- ▶ **Components.** How are the projects and other program components configured to deliver the program and the intended benefits?

- ▶ **Risks and issues.** What are the initial risks, opportunities, and issues identified?

- ▶ **Timeline.** What is the total length of the program, including all key milestone dates?

- ▶ **Resources needed.** What are the estimated program costs and resource needs, such as staff, training, travel, etc.?

- ▶ **Stakeholder considerations.** Who are the key stakeholders and what are the initial strategies to engage them? This information contributes to the development of the communications management plan. (See Section 3.5 for more information on stakeholder engagement.)

- ▶ **Governance framework.** What is the recommended governance structure to manage, control, and support the program? What are the recommended governance structures to guide and oversee the program components, including reporting requirements? What authorities does the program manager possess? How is this information updated in the program governance plan? (See Section 3.6 for more information about governance frameworks.)

The program charter formally expresses the organization's vision, mission, and benefits expected to be produced by the program; it also defines program-specific goals and objectives in alignment with the organization's strategic plan in support of the business case. The program charter provides the program manager with the authority for leading other subsidiary programs, projects, and related activities to be initiated, in addition to the framework by which these program components will be managed and monitored during the course of the program. The program charter is one of the document deliverables that will be used to measure program success. It may also include the metrics for success, a method for measurement, and a clear definition of success.

3.3.3 PROGRAM MANAGEMENT PLAN

A program management plan is a document that integrates the program's subsidiary plans and establishes the management controls and overall plan for integrating and managing the program's individual components. While planning the program, the program manager analyzes available information about the organization's strategic goals and objectives, internal and external influences, program drivers, and the benefits that stakeholders expect the program to realize. The program is defined in terms of expected outcomes, required resources, and strategy for delivering the needed changes to implement new capabilities across the organization.

The program management plan outlines major program events for the purposes of planning and the development of more detailed schedules. The program management plan also reflects the pace at which benefits are realized through the delivery of capabilities and serves as a basis for transition and integration of new capabilities. The program management plan should be continually updated in response to changes in the program's internal and external environments, as well as the program life cycle.

The program roadmap (see Figure 3-3), a major component of the program management plan, is a chronological representation of a program's intended direction, graphically depicting dependencies between major milestones and decision points and reflecting the linkage between the organizational strategy and the program work.

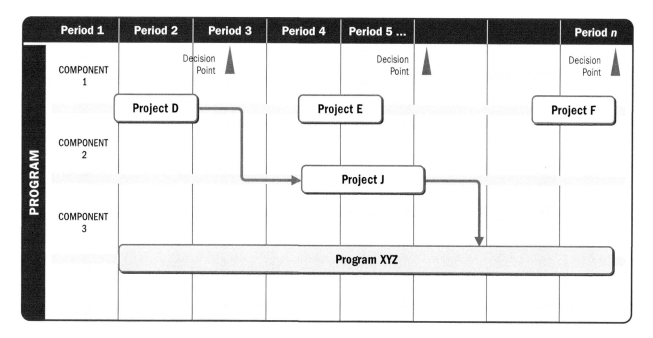

Figure 3-3. Program Roadmap Example

The contents of the program management plan generally consist of the following information:

▶ **Strategic alignment.** Linkage between strategic goals and program components.

▶ **Executive ownership.** A group or person responsible for benefits realization.

▶ **Key milestones.** Significant points or events for making decisions and delivering benefits.

▶ **List of components.** Subsidiary programs, projects, and program-related activities.

▶ **Component information.** Component name, planned period (start and end), and targeted outcomes/benefits.

▶ **Dependencies.** Connections across program components and benefits to create synergy.

▶ **Benefits realization period.** How benefits are fully realized over time.

▶ **Benefits transition and sustainment period.** When benefits make the transition from the programmatic to the operational levels.

The program management plan can be a valuable tool for managing the organization of a program and for assessing a program's progress toward achieving its expected benefits. To better enable governance of the program, the program management plan can be used to show how benefits are delivered within major stages or milestones; it may also include the component details, their durations, and contributions to benefits. In a large construction program, for example, the program management plan may present stages toward the final benefits of the program. In a system development and production program, the program management plan may depict how benefits, such as system capabilities, will be delivered through incremental releases or a series of models. A program management plan is an effective way to communicate the overarching plan and benefits to stakeholders to build and maintain advocacy. The program management plan may be updated throughout the life cycle of the program.

3.3.4 ENVIRONMENTAL ASSESSMENTS

There are often internal and external influences on the program that have a significant impact on its success. Influences from outside the program may be internal to the larger organization or come from external sources. Program managers should identify these influences and take them into account when managing the program in order to ensure ongoing stakeholder alignment, the program's continued alignment with the organization's strategic goals and objectives, and overall program success.

3.3.4.1 Enterprise Environmental Factors

Enterprise environmental factors (EEFs) external to the program may influence the selection, design, funding, and management of a program. Enterprise environmental factors are conditions, not under the immediate control of the team, that influence, constrain, or direct the project, program, or portfolio. A program should be selected and prioritized according to how well it supports the organization's strategic goals and objectives. Strategic goals change, however, in response to EEFs. When this occurs, a change in the direction of the organization may cause the program to be misaligned with the organization's revised strategic plan. In this case, the program may be changed, put on hold, or canceled, regardless of how well it is performing.

Enterprise environmental factors may include but are not limited to:

▶ Business environment;

▶ Force majeure;

▶ Market;

▶ Funding;

▶ Resources;

▶ Industry;

▶ Health, safety, and environment;

▶ Economy;

▶ Cultural diversity;

▶ Geographic diversity;

▶ Regulatory;

▶ Legislative;

▶ Growth;

▶ Supply base;

▶ Technology;

▶ Political influence;

▶ Audit;

▶ New business processes, standards, and practices; and

▶ Discoveries and inventions.

Consideration of these factors and their associated uncertainty or change helps the ongoing assessment and evolution of an organization and the alignment of its programs with its goals. The ongoing management of a program should commit to continual monitoring of the EEFs to ensure the program remains aligned with the organization's strategic objectives.

3.3.4.2 Environmental Analysis

There are various forms of analysis that may be used to assess the validity of a program's business case and program management plan. Consideration of the results from one or more environmental analyses enables the program manager to highlight factors that could potentially impact the program. Representative examples of environmental analyses that may be performed or commissioned by the program manager may include comparative advantage analysis, feasibility studies, SWOT (strengths, weaknesses, opportunities, threats) analysis, assumptions analysis, and historical information analysis. These examples are not intended to be comprehensive or all-inclusive.

3.3.5 PROGRAM RISK MANAGEMENT STRATEGY

Successful delivery of the program management plan, aligned with organizational strategy, and with consideration to the environmental factors found in the environmental assessments, depends on a well-defined program risk strategy.

While Section 4.3.11 details the program risk management activities, this section addresses the specific program risk management strategy (risk threshold, initial program risk assessment, risk response strategy) that drives the program risk management activities (actively identifying, monitoring, analyzing, accepting, mitigating, avoiding, or retiring program risk) to ensure the program is aligned with organizational strategy.

3.3.5.1 Risk Management for Strategic Alignment

Strategic alignment comprises the alignment of the program management plan and its supported objectives to organizational strategy. Obtaining this strategic alignment involves having a risk management strategy that ensures effective management of any risk that can cause the program to be out of alignment with organizational strategy. Such a risk management strategy includes defining program risk thresholds, performing the initial program risk assessment, and developing a high-level program risk response strategy, as well as determining how risks will be communicated to strategic levels of the organization. Strategic alignment requires program risk thresholds to take into account the organization's strategy, including its organizational risk appetite and risk threshold, which is an assessment of the organization's willingness to accept and deal with risks (see Appendix X1.9).

3.3.5.2 Program Risk Thresholds

Risk threshold is the measure of the degree of acceptable variation around a program objective that reflects the risk appetite of the organization and program stakeholders. Establishing program risk thresholds is an integral step in linking program risk management to strategic alignment, and therefore should be done as part of early planning and revisited throughout the program to ensure that program risk thresholds are aligned with any changes at the organizational level.

As previously mentioned, a key element of program risk strategy is the establishment and monitoring of program risk thresholds. Examples of program risk thresholds include:

▶ Minimum level of risk exposure for a risk to be included in the risk register,

▶ Qualitative (e.g., high, medium, low) or quantitative (e.g., numerical) definitions of risk rating, and

▶ Maximum level of risk exposure that can be managed within the program beyond which an escalation is triggered.

Establishing program risk thresholds is an integral step in linking program risk management to strategic alignment and therefore should be done as part of early planning. Based on the risk appetite of the organization and the governance framework, and in collaboration with corporate governance and the program management team, the program manager may also be responsible for ensuring that program risk thresholds are established and observed in the program (see Section 3.6.1.5).

3.3.5.3 Initial Program Risk Assessment

While program risk management (see Section 4.3.11) is conducted throughout the life of the program, the initial program risk assessment, prepared during program definition, offers a unique opportunity to identify risks to organizational strategic alignment. It enables risk to be considered when developing the program management plan and when examining environmental factors. Such an assessment will also include root causes. This will help to develop an appropriate risk-response plan and give priority to deal with critical risks. In addition, it is crucial that the initial program risk assessment identifies any risk to strategic alignment, which includes but is not limited to any uncertain events or conditions that, if they occur, could lead to:

- ▶ Program objectives that are not supportive of organizational objectives,
- ▶ Program management plan that is not aligned with organizational plans,
- ▶ Program management plan that is not supportive of the portfolio management plan,
- ▶ Program objectives that are not supportive of portfolio objectives,
- ▶ Program resource requirements that are out of sync with organizational capacity and capability, and
- ▶ Program benefits that are not realized.

Once the initial program risk assessment is performed, a risk response strategy is developed to complete the program risk management strategy.

3.3.5.4 Program Risk Response Strategy

A program risk response strategy combines the elements of the risk thresholds and initial risk assessment into a plan for how risks will be managed throughout the life of the program. For each identified risk, the risk thresholds can be used to identify the specific response strategy based on a number of rating criteria.

A robust program risk management strategy comprises a specific risk response strategy for each of the risk rating levels that have been developed to reflect the program's risk thresholds.

Once established, the program risk management strategy drives consistency and effectiveness in program risk management activities throughout the program as part of program integration (see Section 4.1) and supporting activities (see Section 4). In addition, the established program risk management strategy enables the program to communicate and manage risks consistently throughout the course of the program performance as part of the governance framework (see Section 4.3.11).

3.3.6 INTERACTIONS WITH PROGRAM MANAGEMENT PRINCIPLES AND OTHER PROGRAM MANAGEMENT PERFORMANCE DOMAINS

The Strategic Alignment performance domain is the foundation of program governance, ensuring that an organization deploys its resources in an optimal manner. It represents a team effort as it is initiated during the program definition phase with the development of the business case, program charter, and program management plan—and is supported with inputs from environmental assessments and program risk management strategy. This synergistic, upstream effort results in the creation of a program management plan that is aligned with organizational goals, objectives, and benefits.

Critical elements of the Strategic Alignment performance domain include the framework, functions, and processes by which a program is monitored, managed, and supported in order to meet organizational strategic and operational goals. This domain also promotes a structured approach to blend project and program management performance domains to enable the program to achieve and optimize its full capabilities. In doing so, Strategic Alignment encompasses the Synergy and Governance program management principles as well as the Benefits Management, Life Cycle Management, Collaboration, Governance Framework, and Stakeholder Engagement performance domains (see Figure 2-1).

3.4 BENEFITS MANAGEMENT

Benefits Management is the program management performance domain that defines, creates, optimizes, delivers, and sustains the benefits provided by the program.

This section includes:

3.4.1 Benefits Identification

3.4.2 Benefits Analysis and Planning

3.4.3 Benefits Delivery

3.4.4 Benefits Transition

3.4.5 Benefits Sustainment

3.4.6 Interactions with Program Management Principles and Other Program Management Performance Domains

The Benefits Management performance domain comprises a number of elements that are central to program success. Benefits management includes processes to clarify the program's planned benefits and intended outcomes, and includes processes for monitoring the program's ability to deliver against these benefits and outcomes. (See more information about benefits and the governance framework in Section 3.6.)

The purpose of benefits management is to focus program stakeholders (such as the program sponsors, program manager, project managers, program teams, program steering committee, and others) on the benefits and outcomes to be provided by the various activities conducted during the program's duration. To do this, the program manager employs benefits management in order to continually:

▶ Identify and assess the value of program benefits,

▶ Manage the interdependencies among the outputs being delivered by the various components within the program,

▶ Analyze the potential impact of planned program changes on the expected benefits,

- ▶ Make sure the expected benefits are aligned with the organization's strategic goals and objectives, and

- ▶ Assign responsibility and accountability for the realization, transition, and sustainment of benefits provided by the program and ensure that the benefits can be sustained.

Benefits are the gains realized by the organization and beneficiaries through portfolio, program, or project outputs and resulting outcomes. Some benefits are relatively certain, easily quantifiable, and may include concrete or finite conditions such as the achievement of an organization's financial objectives (e.g., a 20% increase in revenue or gross margin) or the creation of a physical product or service for consumption or utility. Other benefits may be less quantifiable, tangible or intangible, and may produce somewhat uncertain outcomes. Benefits may also be limited to compliance, avoidance of fines, and avoidance of adverse publicity. For example, regulatory changes may require the initiation of a program in which the realized benefits from regulatory compliance programs may be harder to identify or quantify. Other examples of less tangible program outcomes may include an improvement in employee morale or customer satisfaction, or the reduced incidence of a health condition or disease.

Various types of benefits may be defined and generated by programs. Some benefits, such as expanded market presence, improved financial performance, or operational efficiencies, may be realized by the sponsoring organization, whereas other program outcomes may be realized as benefits by the organization's customers or the program's intended beneficiaries. Each benefit should have an associated beneficiary, whether the benefit is tangible or intangible.

Customers and beneficiaries may be in operational or functional areas within the performing organization, or may be external to the performing organization such as a specific group of interested parties, a business sector, an industry, a particular demographic, or the general population.

Benefits are often defined in the context of the intended beneficiary and may be shared among multiple stakeholders. While the organization's customers or the program's intended beneficiaries may be improved in some way as a result of the program, the performing organization may also benefit from the new or improved capability to consistently deliver and sustain the resulting products, services, or capabilities. Other organizations, stakeholders, and intended beneficiaries may not realize a benefit from the program and may be subject to negative impacts.

Programs and their components deliver outcomes that provide benefits supporting the organization's strategic goals and objectives. Benefits may not be realized until the completion of the program (or well after completion), or may be realized in an iterative fashion as the components within the program produce incremental results that can be leveraged by the intended recipients. Following program closure, benefits may continue to be realized.

Depending on the nature of the program, the program management plan can include graphical representations of the incremental benefits to provide a visual of when the return on investment may help fund the future program benefits and outcomes. As incremental benefits are being produced, the intended recipients, whether internal or external to the organization, are prepared for the resulting change and able to sustain the incremental benefits through to completion of the program and beyond.

Some programs deliver benefits only after all of the components have been completed. In this case, the components' deliverables and outcomes all contribute to the full realization of the full benefit. Examples of programs that deliver the intended benefits at the end of the program may include major construction efforts; public works programs such as roads, dams, or bridges; aerospace programs; aircraft manufacturing or shipbuilding; and medical devices and pharmaceuticals.

Benefits management also ensures that the benefits provided by the organization's investment in a program can be sustained following the conclusion of the program. Throughout the program delivery phase (see Section 3.8.2), program components are planned, developed, integrated, and managed to facilitate the delivery of the intended program benefits. During the program benefits delivery phase, the benefits analysis and planning activities, along with the benefits delivery activities, may be performed in an iterative fashion, especially when corrective action is required to achieve the program benefits.

Program benefits should be monitored, managed, and considered an essential part of the program's deliverables. A risk structure for the benefits should be established based on the organization's risk appetite and the program's strategic value. Each program benefit should be assigned a risk probability. Several factors may drive the probability, including the number of components needed to realize the benefit or the ability of the organization to absorb the change and sustain it.

The Benefits Management performance domain requires continuous interaction with the other program management performance domains throughout the program's duration. Interactions are cyclical in nature and generally begin top-down during early phases of the program and bottom-up in later phases. For example, Strategic Alignment, in conjunction with Stakeholder Engagement, provides the critical inputs and parameters to the program, including vision, mission, strategic goals and objectives, and the business case that defines the program benefits. Program performance data are evaluated through program governance to ensure the program will produce its intended benefits and outcomes.

Figure 3-4 shows the relationship between the program life cycle (see Section 3.8) and the Benefits Management performance domain.

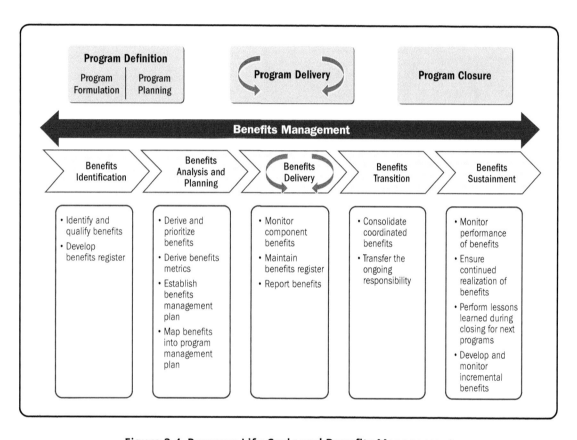

Figure 3-4. Program Life Cycle and Benefits Management

3.4.1 BENEFITS IDENTIFICATION

The purpose of benefits identification is to analyze the available information about organizational and business strategies, internal and external influences, and program drivers to identify and qualify the benefits that program stakeholders expect to realize. As described in Section 3.3.1, organizational initiatives are identified and documented during an organization's strategic planning exercise. These initiatives describe the goals and activities for the organization. A strategic decision-making body, typically in the form of a portfolio management body when within a portfolio structure or governing body for stand-alone programs, may issue a program charter defining the strategic objectives that the program is intended to address and the benefits that are expected to be realized. The program charter is supported by a validated business case. Activities that make up benefits identification include defining the objectives and critical success factors for the program as well as identifying and quantifying organizational benefits.

The business case can serve as a formal declaration of the program benefits, their expected delivery, and the justification for the resources that will be expended to deliver them. The business case establishes the authority, intent, philosophy of the business need, and program sponsorship, while providing direction for the structure, guiding principles, and organization of the program. The program's business case connects with the organizational strategy and objectives, and helps identify the level of investment and support required to achieve the program benefits. See Sections 3.3.1, 3.6.1.3, and 3.8.1.1 for further information on the program business case.

3.4.1.1 Benefits Register

The benefits register collects and lists the planned benefits for the program and is used to measure and communicate the delivery of benefits throughout the duration of the program. In the benefits identification phase, the benefits register is developed based on the program business case, the organization's strategic plan, and other relevant program documents and objectives. The register is then reviewed with key stakeholders to develop the appropriate performance measures for each of the benefits. Key performance indicators are identified in this phase and their associated quantitative and qualitative measures are defined and elaborated in the next phase, where the program benefits register is updated. The benefits register may take many forms but typically includes, at a minimum:

- ▶ List of planned benefits, benefits planned per period (ideally, quantitatively), and benefits achieved (ideally, quantitatively);

- ▶ Mapping of the planned benefits to the program components, as reflected in the program management plan;

- ▶ Description of how each benefit will be measured;

- ▶ Key performance indicators and thresholds for evaluating their achievement;

- ▶ Risk assessment and probability for achieving the benefit;

- ▶ Status or progress indicator for each benefit;

- ▶ Target dates and milestones for benefits achievement; and

- ▶ Person, group, or organization responsible for delivering each benefit.

3.4.2 BENEFITS ANALYSIS AND PLANNING

The purpose of the benefits analysis and planning phase is to establish the benefits management plan and develop the benefits metrics and framework for monitoring and controlling both the components and the measurement of benefits within the program. Activities that make up benefits analysis and planning include:

- ▶ Establishing the benefits management plan that will guide the work throughout the remainder of the program;

- ▶ Defining and prioritizing program benefits, as well as components and their interdependencies;

- ▶ Defining the key performance indicators required to monitor the delivery of program benefits; and

- ▶ Updating positive and negative risks to benefits as more information becomes known.

It is especially important to quantify the incremental delivery of benefits so the realization of planned benefits can be measured during the program. Meaningful measures help the program manager and stakeholders determine whether benefits exceed their control thresholds and whether they are delivered in a timely manner, as illustrated in Figure 3-5. In this example, program costs may continue after program closeout as operational costs to sustain the benefits included in the program funding; program costs may also end at program closeout. When the program continues, it may or may not provide additional funds to the organization accepting the benefit to cover the deferred costs of new benefits; in some cases, the organization may have to self-fund the costs. In addition, quantifiable benefits have not yet exceeded program costs in this example; program benefits are expected to exceed program costs over the time, as specified in the business case.

As the program's benefits are further defined, current risks to these benefits should be further refined and new risks quantified. Examples of risks to implementing benefits include stakeholder acceptance, transition complexity, the amount of change being absorbed by the organization, realization of unexpected outcomes, and other situations that specific industries may encounter. Positive risks in the form of opportunities to optimize the delivery of benefits should also be identified, refined, and quantified. Opportunities may include optimization of how critical resources are allocated or consumed by the program components, or leveraging a new technology to reduce the effort or resources required to deliver a particular benefit.

Program governance empowers the program team to determine if benefits achievement is occurring within the stated parameters, so changes to the components or the program as a whole may be proposed when necessary. Such an analysis requires linking benefits to program objectives, financial expenditures (operational and capital), measurement criteria (including key performance indicators), and measurement and review points. The benefits management plan is also used during the benefits delivery phase to verify that benefits are being realized as planned, while providing feedback to the program steering committee or the authorized body facilitating successful benefits delivery.

Figure 3-5 illustrates how meaningful measures help program managers and stakeholders determine whether benefits exceed their control thresholds and whether they are delivered in a timely manner.

The Standard for Program Management

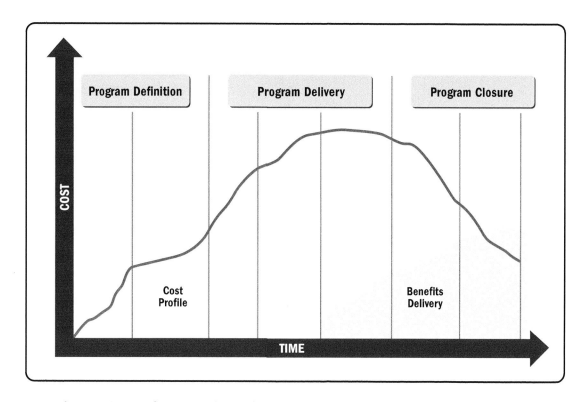

Figure 3-5. Sample Cost and Benefit Profiles across the Generic Program Life Cycle

3.4.2.1 Benefits Management Plan

The benefits management plan formally documents the activities necessary for achieving the program's planned benefits. It identifies how and when benefits are expected to be delivered to the organization and specifies mechanisms that should be in place to ensure the benefits are fully realized over time. The benefits management plan is the baseline document that guides the delivery of benefits during the program's performance. It also identifies the associated activities, processes, and systems needed for the change driven by the realization of benefits; the required changes to existing processes and systems; and how and when the transition to an operational state will occur.

The benefits management plan should:

- ▶ Define each benefit and associated assumptions;
- ▶ Determine how each benefit will be achieved;
- ▶ Link component outputs, outcomes, objectives, and key results to benefits;
- ▶ Define the metrics, including key performance indicators and procedures, to measure benefits;
- ▶ Define roles and responsibilities required to manage the benefits;
- ▶ Define how the resulting benefits and capabilities will be transitioned into an operational state to achieve benefits;
- ▶ Define how the resulting capabilities of benefits will be transitioned to the individuals, groups, or organizations responsible for sustaining the benefits;
- ▶ Provide a process for managing the overall benefits management effort; and
- ▶ Provide a process for removing a benefit that was initially planned but is no longer needed.

3.4.2.2 Benefits Management and the Program Roadmap

Benefits management establishes the program architecture that maps how the components will deliver the capabilities and outcomes that are intended to achieve the program benefits. The program roadmap defines the structure of the program components by identifying the relationships among the components and the rules that govern their inclusion. The program roadmap describes evolving aspects of the program, including incremental benefits delivery. (See Section 3.3.3 for further information on the program roadmap.)

3.4.2.3 Benefits Register Update

The benefits register, initiated during benefits identification, is updated during benefits analysis and planning. At this time, program benefits are mapped to the program components based on the program management plan. The benefits register is then reviewed with the appropriate stakeholders to define and approve key performance indicators and other measures that will be used to manage program performance.

3.4.3 BENEFITS DELIVERY

The purpose of the benefits delivery phase is to ensure that the program delivers the expected benefits, as defined in the benefits management plan. As the program is implemented, risks affecting benefits may be realized, updated, or become obsolete; additionally, new risks and updated ones should be included in the benefits register with the associated benefits. Activities that make up benefits delivery include:

▶ Monitoring the organizational environment (including internal and external factors), program objectives, and benefits realization to ensure the program remains aligned with the organization's strategic objectives;

▶ Initiating, performing, transitioning, and closing components, and managing the interdependencies among them;

▶ Evaluating opportunities and threats affecting benefits, including updating the benefits register for new opportunities and risks affecting benefits, and updating realized or obsolete risks affecting benefits;

▶ Evaluating key performance indicators related to program financials, compliance, quality, safety, and stakeholder satisfaction, in order to monitor the delivery of benefits; and

▶ Recording program progress in the benefits register and reporting to key stakeholders, as directed in the program communications management plan.

The benefits delivery phase ensures there is a defined set of reports or metrics reported to the program management office, program steering committee, program sponsors, and other program stakeholders. By consistently monitoring and reporting on benefits metrics, stakeholders can assess the overall health of the program and take appropriate action to ensure successful benefits delivery.

Benefits management is an iterative process. Benefits analysis and planning and benefits delivery, in particular, have a cyclical relationship. Benefits analysis and planning may be continuously revisited as conditions change. Corrective action may need to be taken in response to information gained from monitoring the organizational environment. Components may have to be modified in order to maintain alignment of the expected program results with the organization's strategic objectives. Corrective action may also need to be taken as a result of evaluating program risks and key performance indicators. Components may require modification due to performance related to program financials, compliance, quality, safety, or stakeholder satisfaction. These corrective actions may require that program components be added, changed, or terminated during the benefits delivery phase.

3.4.3.1 Benefits and Program Components

Each component should be initiated at the appropriate time in the program and integrated to incorporate its output within the program as a whole. The initiation and closure of these components are milestones in the program management plan and schedule. The milestones signal the achievement and delivery of incremental benefits. As the benefits management plan is modified to reflect changes in program pacing, the program management plan (see Section 3.3.3) is also updated.

3.4.3.2 Benefits and Governance Framework

For a benefit to have value, it needs to be realized as described in the benefits management plan, and in a timely manner. The actual benefits delivered by the program components or program itself should be regularly evaluated against the expected benefits, as defined in the benefits management plan. A key aspect to consider is whether program components, and even the program as a whole, are still viable. Should the program's benefit proposition change, such as if the overall life cycle cost exceeds the proposed benefits, or if the benefits are delivered too late, such as when a window of opportunity no longer exists, the program management plan should be assessed. Opportunities to optimize the program pacing may also be identified, as well as other synergies and efficiencies among components. The benefits management plan may have to be modified to reflect changes in the program components and pacing. When the benefits management plan is modified, the program management plan should be updated as well.

The Governance Framework performance domain integrates with the Benefits Management performance domain to help ensure that the program is continuously aligned with the organizational strategy and that the intended value can still be achieved by the delivery of program benefits.

Governance assists in the delivery of promised outcomes for the organization to realize intended benefits. The resulting benefits review requires analysis of the planned versus actual benefits across a wide range of factors, including the key performance indicators. In particular, the following aspects should be analyzed and assessed during the benefits delivery phase:

▶ **Strategic alignment.** Focuses on ensuring the linkage of enterprise and program management plans; on defining, maintaining, and validating the program value proposition; and on aligning program management with enterprise operations management. For internally focused programs, the benefits realization processes measure how the new benefits affect the flow of operations of the organization as the change is introduced, and how negative impacts and the potential disruptiveness of introducing the change may be minimized.

▶ **Value delivery.** Focuses on ensuring the program delivers the intended benefits. There may be a window of opportunity for the realization of a particular planned benefit and for that benefit to generate the desired value. The program manager, program steering committee, and key stakeholders may determine if the window of opportunity was met or compromised by actual events in the program or components, such as a delay, cost overrun, or scope reduction. Investments may also have time value, where shifts in component schedules have additional financial impact.

3.4.4 BENEFITS TRANSITION

The purpose of the benefits transition phase is to ensure that program benefits are transitioned to operational areas and can be sustained once they are transferred. Value is delivered when the organization, community, or other program beneficiaries can utilize these benefits.

Activities included in benefits transition are:

▶ Verifying that the integration, transition, and closure of the program and its components meet or exceed the benefits realization criteria established to achieve the program's strategic objectives; and

▶ Developing a transition plan to facilitate the ongoing realization of benefits when turned over to the impacted operational areas.

Benefits transition ensures that the scope of the transition is defined, the stakeholders in the receiving organizations or functions are identified and participate in the planning, the program benefits are measured and sustainment plans are developed, and the transition is executed.

Benefits transition planning activities within the program are only one part of the complete transition process. The receiving organization or function is responsible for all preparation processes and activities within their domain to ensure the product, service, or capability is received and incorporated into the domain. There may be multiple transition events as individual program components close or as other work activity within the program closes.

Benefits may be realized before the formal work of the program has ended, and can continue long after the formal work has been completed. Benefits transition may be performed following the closure of an individual program component if that component is intended to provide incremental benefits to the organization. Benefits transition may also occur following the closure of the overall program when the program as a whole is intended to provide benefits to the organization and no incremental benefits have been identified.

Benefits are quantified so their realization can be measured over time. Benefits are sometimes not realized until long after the end of active work on a program and may need to be monitored well after the program has closed. At the end of the program, the resulting benefits should be compared against those intended in the business case to ensure that the program will actually deliver the intended benefits.

Benefits transition activities ensure that individual program component results or outputs meet acceptance criteria, are satisfactorily closed or integrated into other program elements, and contribute to the overall achievement of the collective set of program benefits. Benefits transition activities may include but are not limited to:

▶ Evaluation of program and program component performance against applicable acceptance criteria, including key performance indicators;

▶ Review and evaluation of acceptance criteria applicable to delivered components or outputs;

▶ Review of operational and program process documentation;

▶ Review of training and maintenance materials;

- ▶ Review of applicable contractual agreements;

- ▶ Assessment to determine if resulting changes have been successfully integrated;

- ▶ Activities related to optimizing acceptance of resulting changes such as workshops, meetings, training, and other similar activities;

- ▶ Transfer of risk(s) affecting the benefits transitioned to the receiving organization;

- ▶ Readiness assessment and approval by the receiving person, group, or organization; and

- ▶ Disposition of all related resources.

The receiver in the transition process varies depending on the individual component event and program type. A product support organization could be the receiver for a product line that a company develops. For a service provided to customers, the receiver could be the service management organization. If the work products are developed for an external customer, the transition could be to the customer's organization. In some cases, the transition may be from one program to another.

A program may also be closed or terminated with no transition to operations. This situation may occur when the charter is fulfilled and operations are not necessary to continue realization of ongoing benefits, or the chartered program is no longer of value to the organization. Transition may be a formal activity among functions within a single organization or a contract-based activity with an entity outside the organization. The receiving entity should have a clear understanding of the capabilities or results to be transitioned and what is required for the entity to successfully sustain the benefits. All pertinent documents, training and materials, supporting systems, facilities, and personnel should be provided during the transition and may include transition meetings and conferences.

Should any remaining risks affecting the transitioned benefit remain open, the program manager should transfer the risks to the appropriate organization. The organization accepting the benefit may not be the team to monitor ongoing risk for the benefit. The risks may be monitored by a governance organization such as a program management office.

3.4.5 BENEFITS SUSTAINMENT

The purpose of the benefits sustainment phase is the ongoing maintenance activities performed beyond the end of the program by receiving organizations to ensure continued generation of the improvements and outcomes delivered by the program. As the program is closed, responsibility for sustaining the benefits provided by the program may pass to another organization or another program. Benefits may be sustained through operations, maintenance, new components, or other efforts. A benefits sustainment plan should be developed prior to program closure to identify the risks, processes, measures, metrics, and tools necessary to ensure the continued realization of the benefits delivered.

Ongoing sustainment of program benefits should be planned by the program manager and the component project managers during the performance of the program. The actual work that ensures the sustainment of benefits is typically conducted after the close of the program and is beyond the scope of the individual components. Although the receiving person, organization, or beneficiary group performs the work that ensures benefits continue beyond the end of the program, the program manager is responsible for planning these post-transition activities during the performance of the program.

The responsibility for benefits sustainment falls outside the traditional project life cycle; this responsibility, however, may remain within the program life cycle. While these ongoing product, service, or capability support activities may fall within the scope of the program, they typically are operational in nature and not usually run as a program or project.

Activities that make up benefits sustainment include but are not limited to:

▶ Planning for the operational, financial, and behavioral changes necessary for program recipients (individuals, groups, organizations, industries, and sectors) to continue monitoring performance;

▶ Implementing the required change efforts to ensure that the capabilities provided during the course of the program continue when the program is closed and the program's resources are returned to the organization;

▶ Monitoring the performance of the product, service, capability, or results from a reliability and availability-for-use perspective and comparing actual performance to planned performance, including key performance indicators;

- ▶ Monitoring the continued suitability of the deployed product, service, capability, or results to provide the benefits expected by the customers owning and operating it. This monitoring may include the continued viability of interfaces with other products, services, capabilities, or results and the continued completeness of the functionality;

- ▶ Monitoring the continued availability of logistics support for the product, service, capability, or results in light of technological advancements and the willingness of vendors to continue to support older configurations;

- ▶ Responding to customer inputs on their needs for product, service, capability, or results of support assistance or for improvements in performance or functionality;

- ▶ Providing on-demand support for the product, service, capability, or results either in features, improved technical information, or real-time help desk support;

- ▶ Planning for and establishing operational support of the product, service, capability, or results separate from the program management function without relinquishing the other product support functions;

- ▶ Updating technical information concerning the product, service, capability, or improvement in response to frequent product support queries;

- ▶ Planning the transition of the product or capability support from program management to an operations function within an organization;

- ▶ Planning the retirement and phaseout of the product or capability, or the cessation of support with appropriate guidance to the current customers;

- ▶ Developing business cases and the potential initiation of new projects or programs to respond to operational issues with the deployed product, service, or capability being supported or public acceptance/reaction to the improvement or to legislative changes, as well as political, economic, and socioeconomic changes, cultural shifts, or logistics issues with the deployed product, service, capability, or results being supported; and

- ▶ Monitoring any outstanding risks affecting the program's benefits.

Refer to Figure 3-4 for further information regarding the program life cycle and benefits. Benefits management may manifest differently based on different iterative and incremental development approaches. The essence of benefits, which is to capture the gains, is realized by the organization and other stakeholders as the result of outcomes delivered by the program. How that is done and the formality of the process are determined by the participating organization.

3.4.6 INTERACTIONS WITH PROGRAM MANAGEMENT PRINCIPLES AND OTHER PROGRAM MANAGEMENT PERFORMANCE DOMAINS

The Benefits Management performance domain represents numerous components essential to program success. From clearly outlining a program's planned benefits and intended outcomes to determining the program's ability to deliver them, effective management of benefits promotes a harmonious, productive relationship among stakeholders. The result is a potentially long-lasting program that brings great value to an organization.

Through the Benefits Management performance domain, organizations can sustain their competitive advantage and fulfill their purpose through the integration of new products, services, or results that yield benefits. In addition, this performance domain ensures that stakeholder expectations, program benefits, and organizational strategy are interwoven with one another in order to achieve goals and realize benefits. Consequently, Benefits Management aligns with the Benefits Realization and Stakeholders program management principles, and the Collaboration and Stakeholder Engagement performance domains (see Figure 2-1).

3.5 STAKEHOLDER ENGAGEMENT

Stakeholder Engagement is the program management performance domain that identifies and analyzes stakeholder needs and manages expectations and communications to foster stakeholder support.

This section includes:

3.5.1 Program Stakeholder Identification

3.5.2 Program Stakeholder Analysis

3.5.3 Program Stakeholder Engagement Planning

3.5.4 Program Stakeholder Engagement

3.5.5 Program Stakeholder Communications

3.5.6 Interactions with Program Management Principles and Other Program Management Performance Domains

A stakeholder is an individual, group, or organization that may affect, be affected by, or perceive itself to be affected by a decision, activity, or outcome of a project, program, or portfolio.

Stakeholders may be internal or external to the program and may have a positive or negative impact on the outcome of the program. Program and project managers need to be aware of the stakeholders' impacts and levels of influence to understand and address the changing environments of programs and projects.

Stakeholders should be identified, understood, analyzed, prioritized, engaged, and monitored. Unlike program resources, not all stakeholders can be managed directly, but their expectations can be. In many cases, external stakeholders may have more influence than the program manager, program team, or even the program sponsor. Balancing stakeholder interests is important, considering their potential impact on program benefits realization or the inherent conflicting nature of those interests. People have a tendency to resist direct management when the relationship does not have a hierarchical affiliation. For this reason, most program management literature focuses on the notion of stakeholder engagement rather than stakeholder management.

Stakeholder engagement can be expressed as direct and indirect communication among the stakeholders and the program's leaders and team. Engagement with the program team may be performed by people with different roles in the program and project teams. Stakeholder engagement, however, includes more than just communication. For example, stakeholders can be engaged by involving them in goal setting, quality analysis reviews, or other program activities. The primary objective is to gain and maintain stakeholder acceptance for the program's objectives, benefits, and outcomes.

Ambiguity, volatility, and uncertainty are characteristics of complexity, which is an element in many programs. The complexity of those environments warrants the efforts of the program manager to understand and manage the wide stakeholder base. Figure 3-6 depicts a diverse stakeholder environment that may shape the actions needed to manage those expectations. Mapping stakeholders is a pivotal step to ensure successful expectation management, and in turn deliver organizational benefits. Beyond the communications aspect, stakeholder engagement consists of negotiation of objectives, agreement on desired benefits, commitment to resources, and ongoing support throughout the program.

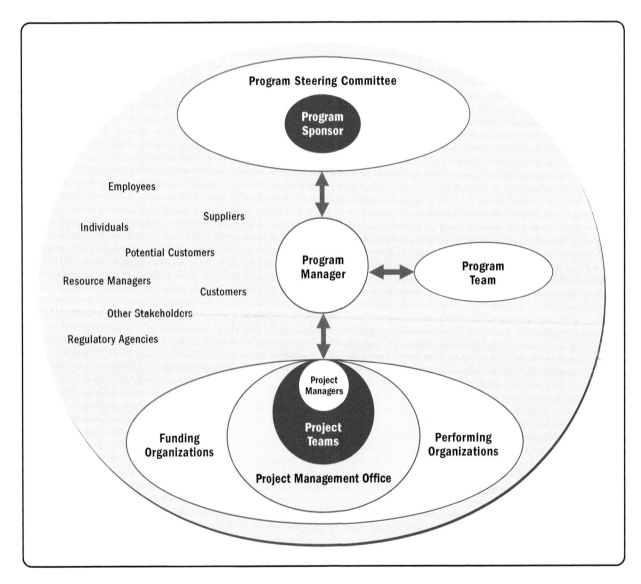

Figure 3-6. Stakeholder Environment for Programs

The level of interest and the level of influence in the program may vary widely from stakeholder to stakeholder. A stakeholder may be unaware of the program and its intended benefits or, if aware, may not support it. It is the responsibility of the program manager to expend sufficient time and energy with known stakeholders to ensure all points of view and risk tolerance have been considered and addressed.

The program manager interacts with stakeholders in the following ways:

▶ Engages stakeholders by assessing their influence, attitudes, availability, and interests toward the program;

▶ Includes stakeholders in program activities and uses communications targeted to their needs, interests, requirements, expectations, and wants, according to their change readiness and selected organizational change management strategy speed and scale;

▶ Monitors stakeholder feedback within the context and understanding of the relationship to the program; and

▶ Supports training initiatives as needed within the context of the program or related organizational structure of the program component.

This two-way communication enables the program manager to deliver benefits for the organization in accordance with the program charter.

Stakeholder engagement at the program level can be challenging because some stakeholders view the program benefits as change. People have the propensity to resist change whenever they have not directly requested it, have not participated in creating it, do not understand the necessity for it, or are concerned with the effect of the change on them personally. Thus, the program manager and program team members need to understand the attitudes and agendas for each stakeholder throughout the duration of the program. The program manager should be the champion for change in the organization and understand the motivations of each stakeholder who could attempt to alter the course of the program, intentionally derail it, or prevent it from realizing one or more of its intended benefits or outcomes. As the program evolves in this complex environment and adapts to ensure that it delivers intended benefits, its strategy and plans may change. For support, the program manager also draws on the program sponsor or sponsoring group to foster organizational conditions, through program governance, to enable the realization of program benefits.

The program manager should bridge the gap between the current state of the organization and the desired future state. To do so, the program manager should understand the current state and how the program and its benefits will move the organization to the future state. Therefore, the program manager should be familiar with organizational change management.

Successful program managers utilize strong leadership skills to set clear stakeholder engagement goals to help the program team address the change the program will bring. These goals include engaging stakeholders to assess their readiness for change, planning for the change, providing program resources and support for the change, facilitating or negotiating the approach to implementing the change, and obtaining and evaluating the stakeholders' feedback on the program's progress.

3.5.1 PROGRAM STAKEHOLDER IDENTIFICATION

Program stakeholder identification aims to systematically identify all key stakeholders (or stakeholder groups) in the stakeholder register. This register lists the stakeholders and categorizes their relationships to the program, their abilities to influence the program outcome, their degrees of support for the program, and other characteristics or attributes the program manager determines could influence the stakeholders' perceptions and the program's outcomes. Table 3-1 provides an example of stakeholder categorization within a program.

Table 3-1. Example Stakeholder Register

Name	Organizational Position	Program Role	Power/ Influence Level	Level of Interest	Communication
Stakeholder 1	Director	Supplier	Keep satisfied	Low	Email monthly
Stakeholder 2	Customer	Recipient	Keep informed	Medium	Conference weekly
Stakeholder 3	Senior vice president	Sponsor	Manage closely	High	Status report quarterly

* This table is an example only, and can be tailored to reflect the unique characteristics of each program.

The stakeholder register should be established and maintained in such a way that members of the program team can reference it easily for use in reporting, distributing program deliverables, and providing formal and informal communications. It should be noted that the stakeholder register may contain politically and legally sensitive information and may have access and review restrictions placed on it by the program manager. As a result, it may be appropriate to ensure that the stakeholder register is properly secured. The program manager should comply with data privacy regulations in countries or localities where the program operates. The stakeholder register is a dynamic document. As the program evolves, new stakeholders may emerge, or interests of current groups may shift. The program manager should monitor both the internal and external environment and prepare and update the register as required.

Examples of key program stakeholders include but are not limited to:

▶ **Program sponsor.** An individual or a group that provides resources and support for the program and is accountable for enabling success. The program sponsor is often the champion of the program, sometimes referred to as a spokesperson or advocate.

▶ **Program steering committee.** A group of participants representing various program-related interests with the purpose of supporting the program under its authority by providing guidance, endorsements, and approvals through governance practices. This committee may be referred to as the program governance board.

▶ **Portfolio manager.** The person or group assigned by the performing organization to establish, balance, monitor, and control portfolio components in order to achieve strategic business objectives.

▶ **Program manager.** The person authorized by the performing organization to lead the team or teams responsible for achieving program objectives. Some teams may not be under the direct authority of the program manager and, therefore, facilitation may be required.

▶ **Project manager.** The person assigned by the performing organization to lead the team that is responsible for achieving the project objectives.

▶ **Program team members.** The individuals performing program activities.

▶ **Project team members.** The individuals performing constituent project activities.

- ▶ **Funding organization.** The part of the organization, or the external organization, providing funding for the program.

- ▶ **Performing organization.** An enterprise whose personnel are the most directly involved in doing the work of the project or program.

- ▶ **Program management office.** A management structure that standardizes the program-related governance processes and facilitates the sharing of resources, methodologies, tools, and techniques.

- ▶ **Customers.** The individuals or organization(s) that will use the new capabilities delivered by the program and derive the anticipated benefits. The customer is a major stakeholder in the program's final result and will influence whether the program is judged to be successful or not.

- ▶ **Potential customers.** The past and future customers who will be watching intently to see how well the program delivers the stated benefits.

- ▶ **Suppliers.** Product and service providers who are contracted or paid to support or execute specific program activities.

- ▶ **Regulatory agencies.** A public authority or government agency responsible for setting and managing the regulatory and legal boundaries of their local and national sovereign governments. Typically, these organizations will set mandatory standards or requirements.

- ▶ **Affected individuals or organizations.** Those who perceive that they will either benefit from, or be disadvantaged by, the program's activities.

- ▶ **Other groups.** Groups representing consumer, environmental, or other interests (including political interests). Organizational support functions, such as human resources, legal, administration, and infrastructure, are also considered key stakeholders.

The identification of stakeholders using the various group techniques—brainstorming or Delphi, for example—aims to name stakeholders across the entire program life cycle. The resulting stakeholder register is an essential tool leading to effective engagement.

3.5.2 PROGRAM STAKEHOLDER ANALYSIS

Once key stakeholders are listed in the stakeholder register, the program manager will categorize them in order to start analyzing them. The categorization will highlight differences in their needs, expectations, or influence. Key information should be obtained from stakeholders to better understand the organizational culture, politics, and concerns related to the program, as well as its overall impact. This information may be obtained through historical information, individual interviews, focus groups, or questionnaires and surveys. Questionnaires and surveys allow the program team to solicit feedback from a greater number of stakeholders than is possible with interviews or focus groups. Regardless of the technique used, key information should be gathered through open-ended questions to elicit stakeholder feedback. From the information gathered, a prioritized list of stakeholders should be developed to help focus the engagement effort on the people and organizations with the most influence (positive or negative) on the program. The program manager should establish and maintain a balance between mitigating the effect of stakeholders who view the program negatively and encouraging and exploiting the active support of the stakeholders who see the overall program as a positive contribution.

For complex programs, the program manager may develop a stakeholder map to visually represent the interactions of stakeholders' current and desired levels of support and influence. The map serves as a tool to assess the impact of a change on the program community. It allows the program team to make informed decisions about how and when to engage stakeholders, taking into account their interest, influence, involvement, interdependencies, and support levels. An alternative classification model used for stakeholder analysis is the power/interest grid. This model groups stakeholders based on their level of authority ("power") and their level of concern ("interest") regarding the program outcomes. Figure 3-7 presents an example of the power/interest grid, with A–H representing the placement of generic stakeholders.

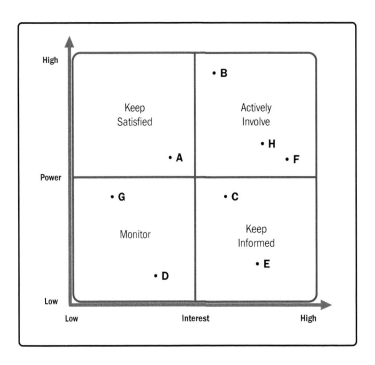

Figure 3-7. Example Power/Interest Grid with Stakeholders

By identifying stakeholder expectations and clearly outlining key indicators and expected benefits, the program manager creates a framework for addressing ongoing program activities and evolving stakeholder needs. The stakeholder map can function as a tool to help identify the need for interactions with stakeholders. It brings to light the potential partnerships among stakeholders and the collaboration opportunities that contribute to the success of the program. As the need arises, the program manager can use the stakeholder map to remind and engage teams about which stakeholders need to be engaged at various times in the program life cycle. The stakeholder register, and the prioritization of stakeholder engagement activities, should be regularly reviewed and updated as the work of the program progresses.

3.5.3 PROGRAM STAKEHOLDER ENGAGEMENT PLANNING

The stakeholder engagement planning activity outlines how all program stakeholders will be engaged throughout the duration of the program. The stakeholder register and stakeholder map are analyzed with consideration of the organization's strategic plan, program charter, and program business case to understand the environment in which the program will operate.

As part of the stakeholder analysis and engagement planning, the following aspects for each stakeholder are taken into consideration:

- ▶ Organizational culture and acceptance of change,
- ▶ Attitudes about the program and its sponsors,
- ▶ Relevant phase(s) applicable to stakeholders' specific engagement,
- ▶ Expectation of program benefits delivery,
- ▶ Degree of support or opposition to the program benefits, and
- ▶ Ability to influence the outcome of the program.

This effort results in the stakeholder engagement plan, which contains a detailed strategy for stakeholder engagement, based on the current situation. The plan includes stakeholder engagement guidelines and provides insight on how the stakeholders are engaged in various components of the program. The plan defines the metrics used to measure the performance of stakeholder engagement activities. The metrics may include measures of participation in meetings and other collaboration channels—and the degree of active or passive support or resistance—and can also strive to measure the effectiveness of the engagement in meeting its intended goal. The guidelines for stakeholder engagement should be provided to the component projects, subsidiary programs, and other program activities. The stakeholder engagement plan provides critical information used in the development of program documentation and its ongoing alignment as stakeholders are added or deleted, or if information about existing stakeholders is modified.

3.5.4 PROGRAM STAKEHOLDER ENGAGEMENT

Stakeholder engagement is a continuous program activity because the list of stakeholders—and their attitudes and opinions—changes as the program progresses and delivers benefits. One of the primary roles of the program manager throughout the duration of the program is to ensure all stakeholders are adequately and appropriately engaged. Identifying stakeholders, mapping their interests, and planning for stakeholder engagement directly support this process. The stakeholder register, stakeholder map, and stakeholder engagement plan should be referenced and evaluated often, and updated as needed.

Interacting and engaging with stakeholders allows the program team to communicate program benefits and their relevance to the organization's strategic objectives. When necessary, the program manager may utilize strong communication, negotiation, and conflict resolution skills to help defuse stakeholder opposition to the program and its stated benefits. Large programs with diverse stakeholders may also require facilitated negotiation sessions among stakeholders or stakeholder groups when their expectations conflict.

To help stakeholders establish common, high-level expectations for the delivery of the program's benefits, the program manager provides stakeholders with appropriate information contained in the program charter and program business case, which can include an accompanying executive brief to summarize the details of the risks, dependencies, and benefits.

The primary metrics for stakeholder engagement are positive contributions to the realization of the program's objectives and benefits, stakeholder participation, and frequency or rate of communication with the program team. The program manager strives to ensure all interactions with the stakeholders are adequately logged, including meeting invitations, attendance, meeting minutes, and action items. Program managers review stakeholder metrics regularly to identify potential risks caused by a lack of participation. These participation trends are analyzed and root cause analysis is performed to identify and address the causes of nonparticipation. The history of stakeholder participation provides important background information that could influence stakeholder perceptions and expectations. For example, when a stakeholder has not been actively participating, it may be that the stakeholder is confident in the program's direction, possibly has inaccurate expectations, or has lost interest in the program. Thorough analysis avoids incorrect assumptions about stakeholder behavior that could lead to unanticipated issues or poor program management decisions.

As the program team works with the stakeholders, it collects and logs stakeholder issues and concerns, managing them to closure. Use of a log to document, prioritize, and track issues helps the entire program team understand the feedback received from stakeholders. When the list of stakeholders is small, a simple spreadsheet may be an adequate tracking tool. For programs with complex risks and issues affecting large numbers of stakeholders, a more sophisticated tracking and prioritization mechanism may be required.

Stakeholder issues and concerns are likely to affect aspects of the program such as its scope, benefits, risks, costs, schedule, priorities, and outcomes. Impact analysis may be used to understand the urgency and probability of stakeholder issues and determine which issues could become program risks.

3.5.5 PROGRAM STAKEHOLDER COMMUNICATIONS

Effective communication creates a bridge between diverse stakeholders who may have different cultural and organizational backgrounds, different levels of expertise, and different perspectives and interests, all of which may impact or influence the delivery of benefits by the program. Communication is at the heart of stakeholder engagement. It is key to executing program endeavors and, ultimately, delivering benefits to the organization. This critical component is a vehicle for information sharing, negotiation, and collaboration among the program team members to drive program implementation efforts.

The program manager and program team should actively engage stakeholders throughout the life cycle of the program, with particular attention paid to those key stakeholders who have a high degree of power and influence. A strategy can be crafted for each stakeholder as identified in the stakeholder register (see Table 3-1). This strategy accounts for communication requirements such as what information should be communicated, including language, format, content, and level of detail. It can also address a feedback loop to discuss program changes and an escalation process. The resulting communication approach targets stakeholder support for the program strategy and delivery of the program benefits.

Some stakeholders are naturally curious about the program and often raise questions. These questions and their answers should be captured and published in a way that allows multiple stakeholders to benefit from the exchange. In many cases, the documentation may need to be formatted and presented differently for certain stakeholder audiences. It is important that decision-making stakeholders are provided with adequate information to make the right choices at the right time to move the program forward. The program manager should continually monitor changes and update stakeholder engagement activities and deliverables as needed.

Communication with some stakeholders is inherent in many program activities; these activities are described in detail in Section 4. Relevant program communications should be recorded and stored as a continuous process by the program manager. The program manager should constantly manage and foster an environment where stakeholder communication needs are met.

3.5.6 INTERACTIONS WITH PROGRAM MANAGEMENT PRINCIPLES AND OTHER PROGRAM MANAGEMENT PERFORMANCE DOMAINS

Although overseen by capable program and project managers, programs reflect the unique knowledge, perspectives, confidence, or uncertainty of their stakeholders. Whether they are individuals or groups of people with a specific focus, stakeholders represent a diversity of viewpoints and capabilities—and they are united by the fact that they could potentially be affected by a decision, activity, or outcome of a portfolio, program, or project. Building and maintaining strong relationships among varied stakeholders is critical to a successful program, and often the difference between business triumph and defeat. Thus, program and project managers should practice effective planning and communications and actively encourage the acceptance of diverse points of view.

A vital aspect of the Stakeholder Engagement performance domain is helping program and project managers smoothly align stakeholder expectations, program risks and benefits, and organizational strategy, while adapting to changes or obstacles. This alignment enables efficient oversight of the program framework, functions, and processes in order to meet strategic and operational goals. As a result, the Stakeholder Engagement performance domain connects with the Stakeholders, Synergy, Leadership, Risk, and Governance program management principles, in addition to the Benefits Management, Collaboration, Governance Framework, Stakeholder Engagement, and Strategic Alignment performance domains (see Figure 2-1).

3.6 GOVERNANCE FRAMEWORK

The Governance Framework performance domain enables and performs program decision-making, establishes practices to support the program, and maintains program oversight.

This section includes:

3.6.1 Governance Framework Practices

3.6.2 Governance Framework Roles

3.6.3 Governance Framework Design and Implementation

3.6.4 Interactions with Program Management Principles and Other Program Management Performance Domains

The Governance Framework performance domain outlines the processes and functions for managing, sustaining, and monitoring a program to meet an organization's strategic and operational goals while delivering anticipated benefits.

A governance framework ensures that oversight is carried out by a review and decision-making group responsible for approving all program recommendations under its purview. This group works closely with the program manager, who oversees daily program activities and ensures the program team understands and adheres to established governance procedures and their underlying governance principles.

Governance of components of a program is often achieved through the actions of the program manager and program team responsible for the integrated outcomes of the program. Such a responsibility may also be called component governance.

The Governance Framework performance domain is impacted by organizational and portfolio governance, which is a structured way to provide control, direction, and coordination through people, policies, and processes to meet organizational strategic and operational goals. Typically, portfolio governance is the hierarchical level of governance where program investments are authorized.

Figure 3-8 illustrates the governance relationships for programs. Within a portfolio structure, portfolio-governance-supporting functions and processes are linked to programs through portfolio governance. For stand-alone programs that are outside of a portfolio structure, a governing body provides governance-supporting functions and processes to programs, including governance policies, oversight, control, integration, and decision-making functions and processes. The type and frequency of the governance activities are determined by portfolio governance and governing bodies. The portfolio, if one exists, provides governance policies, oversight, control, integration, and decision-making functions and processes to programs within the portfolio structure.

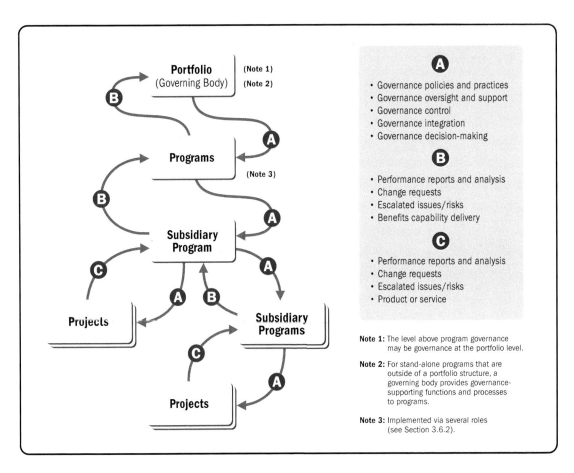

Figure 3-8. Governance Relationships for Programs

An effective governance framework is especially important in environments that are highly complex or uncertain, when it is necessary to respond rapidly to outcomes and information that become available during the course of the program. The Governance Framework performance domain makes it possible to clarify the organization's vision, facilitate alignment of the program with organizational strategy, and enable the periodic balancing of program demands with current organizational capabilities. Governance participants are able to monitor and, as necessary, authorize or limit changes to the activities performed as part of a program. Governance decision forums focus on facilitating the adaptive realignment of the program's approach to enable the delivery of intended benefits. The roles and participants performing governance framework activities are described in Section 3.6.2.

The governance framework provides an important means by which programs seek authorization and support for dynamically changing program strategies or plans in response to emergent outcomes. A program within a portfolio is likely to be governed within the framework of the portfolio. Portfolio governance, as outlined in *The Standard for Portfolio Management* [3], provides the framework, functions, and processes providing oversight, control, integration, and decision-making practices to programs, projects, and operations within the portfolio structure. In the event that the organization does not have portfolios of programs and projects, then the process to develop the idea and steps to authorize the program should be carried out within the organizational governance framework.

3.6.1 GOVERNANCE FRAMEWORK PRACTICES

The governance framework practices that are applicable to program work are detailed in Sections 3.6.1.1 through 3.6.1.10.

3.6.1.1 Program Governance Plan

To facilitate the design and implementation of effective governance, many organizations prepare documented descriptions of each program's governance frameworks, functions, and processes. Such descriptions are summarized in a program governance plan, which may be a stand-alone document or a subsection of the program management plan. While typically there will be a program governance plan for each program in the organization, some organizations may use a single program governance plan to govern several programs.

The purpose of the program governance plan is to describe the systems and methods used to monitor, manage, and support a given program, and the responsibilities of specific roles for ensuring the timely and effective use of those systems and methods. This document is referenced throughout the program's duration to provide and demonstrate that the program is conforming to established governance expectations and agreements. The governance framework may be modified as appropriate, based on outcomes attained during the course of the program. It is generally accepted good practice to ensure that modifications are communicated to those stakeholders responsible for program governance and program management.

3.6.1.2 Governance Framework and Organizational Vision and Goals

The vision and goals of the organization provide the basis for strategic mandates that drive the definitions of most programs. The Governance Framework performance domain ensures that any program within its area of authority defines its vision and goals in order to support those of the organization.

3.6.1.3 Program Approval, Endorsement, and Definition

In most organizations, the governance framework outlines responsibility for approving each program's approach and plan for how it will pursue program and organizational goals, and for authorizing the use of resources to support components and other program work in pursuit of that approach. These approvals occur in the program definition phase and are facilitated, for example, by the program business case or the program charter.

The governance framework facilitates program funding to the degree necessary to support the approved business case. Often, program funding is provided through a budgetary process that is controlled by a group responsible for oversight of several programs. In these instances, program funding is provided in a manner consistent with program needs and organizational priorities, as defined through the organization's portfolio management processes.

When program funding needs to be secured from external sources, the program steering committee is typically responsible for entering into the appropriate agreements necessary to secure it. The funding may have constraints that limit its use due to laws, regulations, or other limitations.

3.6.1.4 Program Monitoring, Reporting, and Controlling

The governance participants are positioned to set the framework for performance management in their pursuit of organizational goals, working collaboratively with the program manager to optimize the benefits by capturing opportunities.

To support the organization's ability to monitor program progress and strengthen the organization's ability to assess program status and conformance with organizational controls, many organizations define standardized reporting and controlling processes applicable to all programs, including earned value management, as outlined in *The Standard for Earned Value Management* [4]. Individuals or groups responsible for the governance framework can assume responsibility for enforcing program compliance with such processes. Reporting and controlling documents may include:

- ▶ Operational status and progress of programs, components, and related activities;
- ▶ Expected or incurred program resource requirements;
- ▶ Known program risks, their response plans, and escalation criteria;
- ▶ Strategic and operational assumptions;
- ▶ Benefits realized and expected sustainment;
- ▶ Decision-making criteria, tracking, and communication, as well as program change control;
- ▶ Compliance with corporate and legal policies (e.g., update on external reporting needs);
- ▶ Program information management;
- ▶ Issues and issue response plans; and
- ▶ Program funding and financial performance.

3.6.1.5 Program Risk and Issue Governance

Risk and issue governance frameworks ensure that key risks and issues are escalated appropriately and addressed in a timely manner. The escalation processes typically operate at two levels:

- ▶ **Internal.** Within the program—among component teams, the program management team, and the program steering committee.

- ▶ **External.** Outside the program—among the program management team, the program's steering committee, subject matter experts, and other stakeholders.

Whether internal or external, program, portfolio, and organizational risks cascade down to the subsidiary programs, projects, and other program components.

It is important to note that program risks can be compounded, as opposed to aggregated, by the program component teams. Essentially, program risks can be bigger than the sum of their parts. The expectations for risk and issue escalation at all levels are documented and communicated to ensure that the organization clearly defines its requirements for the engagement of governing stakeholders at the appropriate times for effective risk and issue management.

Based on the risk appetite of the organization, and working with organizational governance and the program management team, the governance framework may establish program risk thresholds for adherence within the program.

3.6.1.6 Program Quality Governance

The governance of quality is essential to the success of the program. Quality management planning is often performed at the component level and is therefore governed at that level. The governance participants are responsible for reviewing and approving the approach to quality management and the standards by which quality will be measured, documented, and reported. (More details about program quality management activities can be found in Section 4.)

3.6.1.7 Program Change Governance

The governance framework plays a critical role in the authorization of changes to the program. The program steering committee or appropriate body is responsible for defining the types of changes that a program manager would be independently authorized to approve, and those changes that would be significant enough to require further discussion prior to approval. As a result of the monitoring, reporting, and controlling practices, the governance participants should be positioned to assess proposed changes to the program's planned approach or activities.

The program manager assesses whether the risks associated with potential changes are acceptable or desirable, whether the proposed changes are operationally feasible and supportable, and whether the changes are significant enough to require approval of the portfolio management body when a program is within a portfolio structure or suitable governing body for stand-alone programs outside of portfolios. The program manager then recommends changes that require approval by governance participants through the program steering committee. The extent to which a change can be authorized by the program steering committee is bounded by the program business case and organizational strategy. A record of the proposed change, its rationale, and its outcome is maintained by the program team. Section 4.3.4 provides details of the program change governance activity.

3.6.1.8 Governance Framework Reviews

The governance framework endorses reviews of programs at key decision points in the program life cycle. These reviews are conducted at times that coincide with the initiation or completion of significant segments of a program to enable governance to approve or disapprove the passage of a program from one significant segment to another. They also facilitate the review and approval of any required changes to the program at key decision points.

For example, key decision points occur at the end of program phases. Phase gate reviews are reviews at the end of a phase in which a decision is made whether or not to continue to the next phase, continue with modification, or end a program or program component. These reviews enable governance to approve or disapprove the passage of a program from one significant phase to another.

By conducting reviews, the program steering committee has the opportunity to confirm its support for continuation of the program as defined or to initiate recommendations for adaptive changes to the program's strategy, improving the program's ability to pursue and deliver its intended benefits.

Program periodic health checks, generally held between decision point reviews, assess a program's ongoing performance and progress toward the realization and sustainment of benefits. The importance and use of these reviews increase when there is an extended period between scheduled decision point reviews.

At times, decision point reviews may result in termination of the program. Examples of this include times when it is determined, for any number of reasons, that the program is not likely to deliver its expected benefits, cannot be supported at the investment level required, or should no longer be pursued as determined in a portfolio review.

The frequency of program reviews and the specific requirements of those reviews may reflect the autonomy given to the program team to oversee and manage the program. The organization's expectations for governance framework reviews should be detailed in the program governance plan.

3.6.1.9 Program Component Initiation and Transition

Program steering committee approval is required prior to the initiation of individual components of the program to the extent that the initiation of a component requires: (a) the introduction of additional governance structures that are responsible for monitoring and managing the component, and (b) the firm commitment of organizational resources for its completion. The program manager frequently acts as the proposer when seeking authorization for the initiation of these components. The approval of the initiation of a new program component generally includes:

▶ Developing, modifying, or reconfirming the business case;

▶ Ensuring the availability of resources to perform the component;

▶ Defining or reconfirming individual accountabilities for management and pursuit of the component;

▶ Enabling the communication of critical, component-related information to key stakeholders;

▶ Ensuring the establishment of component-specific, program-level quality control plans; and

▶ Authorizing the governance structure to track the component's progress against its goals.

The approach used in managing activities within the component is generally dependent on the specific nature of the component. For example, component projects should be managed according to the principles and practices of project management, as defined in the *PMBOK® Guide* [1], whereas other programs should be managed according to the principles defined and described in this standard.

Upon initiation of a new component, all program-level documentation and records dealing with the component should be updated to reflect any changes to the affected components.

Approval is generally required for transition and closure of an individual program component. The review of any recommendation for the transition or closure of a program component generally includes:

▶ Confirming that the business case for the component has been sufficiently satisfied or that further pursuit of the component's goals should be discontinued,

▶ Ensuring appropriate program-level communications of the component's closure to key stakeholders,

▶ Ensuring component compliance with program-level quality control plans (when required),

▶ Assessing organizational or program-level lessons learned and knowledge transfer as a consequence of performance of the component in transition, and

▶ Confirming that all other accepted practices for project or program transition or closure have been satisfied.

3.6.1.10 Program Closure

The program steering committee reviews and makes decisions on recommendations for the closure of programs. It assesses whether conditions warranting the program are satisfied, and that recommendations for closure of a program are consistent with the current organizational vision, mission, and strategy. Alternatively, programs may be terminated because changes in the organizational strategy or environment have resulted in diminished program benefits or needs. Regardless of the cause for termination, closure procedures should be implemented. Practices and processes commonly used to conduct program closure are described in detail in Section 3.8.

At program closure, the importance of effectively transitioning the program governance to operational governance will directly impact the benefits realized (see Section 3.4). The final program report is approved by the governance participants during closure.

3.6.2 GOVERNANCE FRAMEWORK ROLES

Establishing an appropriate collaborative relationship among individuals responsible for the governance framework and program management is critical to the success of programs in delivering the benefits desired by the organization. Program managers rely on the program steering committee (also referred to as the program governance board, oversight committee, or board of directors) members to establish organizational conditions that enable the effective pursuit of programs and to resolve issues that inevitably arise when the needs of their program conflict with the needs of other programs, projects, or ongoing operational activities.

Establishing a collaborative relationship between the program steering committee and program managers is also critical to the success of the organization. In accordance with the program charter, program managers assume responsibility and accountability for effectively managing programs in the pursuit of organizational goals as authorized by the program steering committee.

Governance framework structures are best defined in a manner that is specific to the needs of each organization and the requirements of the program. A comprehensive governance framework model carefully considers the program and the organizational context in which it is pursued. However, within organizations, the relationship between the governance framework and program management functions is often managed by assigning key roles to individuals who are part of those functions and are recognized as important stakeholders. More details on the factors considered in designing the Governance Framework performance domain are provided in Section 3.6.3.

While the design, participants, and roles fulfilling the governance framework will be specific to the program within an organization, the following roles are commonly used:

▶ **Program sponsor.** An individual or group that provides resources and support to the program and is accountable for enabling success.

▶ **Program steering committee.** A group of participants representing various program-related interests with the purpose of supporting the program under its authority by providing guidance, endorsements, and approvals through the governance practices. Members are typically executives from organizational groups who support the program's components and operations. In some cases, the program sponsor is the chair of the program steering committee.

▶ **Program manager.** The person authorized by the performing organization to lead the team or teams responsible for achieving program objectives. In the context of governance, this role interacts with the program steering committee and sponsor and manages the program to ensure delivery of the intended benefits.

- **Program management office.** A management structure that standardizes the program-related governance processes and facilitates the sharing of resources, methodologies, tools, and techniques.

- **Project manager.** The person assigned by the performing organization to lead the team that is responsible for achieving the project objectives. In the context of governance, this role interacts with the program manager and program sponsor and manages the delivery of the project's product, service, or result.

- **Other stakeholders.** These stakeholders include the manager of the portfolio of which the program is a component, as well as operational managers and product managers receiving the capabilities delivered by the program.

The responsibilities assigned to each of the roles listed are for guidance only. Carrying out the activities of the Governance Framework performance domain will fulfill these responsibilities and the allocation among roles is often dependent on several design factors (see Section 3.6.3).

3.6.2.1 Program Sponsor

The program sponsor is the individual responsible for allocating organizational resources to the program and for program success. The program sponsor role is frequently filled by an executive member of the program steering committee who has a senior role in directing the organization and its investment decisions, and who is personally vested in the success of related organizational programs. In many organizations, the program sponsor acts as the chairperson of the program steering committee and assigns and oversees the progress of the program manager.

Typical responsibilities of the program sponsor include:

- Chairing the program steering committee,

- Securing funding for the program and ensuring program goals and objectives are aligned with the strategic vision,

- Having authority in decision-making related to program management,

- Enabling the delivery of benefits, and

- Removing barriers and obstacles to program success.

As chair or member of the program steering committee, the sponsor is integral to its responsibilities. It is critical that the organization selects an appropriate program sponsor and then allows them to perform the role effectively. Sufficient time and resources should be provided to enable success, which often requires relief from other management and executive duties.

The caliber, experience, and availability of the sponsor impact the effectiveness of the program and, in some cases, are the difference between perceived success and failure. The program sponsor may be required to drive changes throughout the organization so operations can accommodate capabilities delivered by the program, and to secure the available positive benefits and steward the handling of negative benefits. As such, the sponsor is integral to the communication and stakeholder processes. Typically, an effective sponsor exhibits the following attributes:

- ▶ Ability to influence stakeholders,
- ▶ Ability to work across different stakeholder groups to find mutually beneficial solutions,
- ▶ Leadership,
- ▶ Decision-making authority, and
- ▶ Effective communication skills.

3.6.2.2 Program Steering Committee

Most organizations seek to ensure appropriate implementation of the governance framework by establishing program steering committees that are responsible for defining and implementing appropriate governance practices. Program steering committees are usually staffed by individuals who are either individually or collectively recognized as having organizational insight and decision-making authority that are critical to the establishment of program goals, strategy, and operational plans. The program steering committee is chaired by, or has as a member, the program sponsor. Program steering committees are usually composed of executive-level stakeholders who have been selected for their strategic insight, technical knowledge, functional responsibilities, operational accountabilities, responsibilities for managing the organization's portfolio, and abilities to represent important stakeholder groups. Program steering committees may include senior leaders from the functional groups responsible for supporting significant elements of the program, including, for example, the organizational executives and leaders responsible for supporting the program's components. Program steering committees, staffed in this way, improve the likelihood that the activities described in the Governance Framework performance domain will be well positioned to efficiently address issues or questions that may arise during the performance of the program. Program steering committees ensure that programs are pursued in an environment with appropriate organizational knowledge and expertise, well supported by cohesive policies and processes, and empowered by their access to those with decision-making authority.

Typical responsibilities include:

▶ Providing governance support for the program to include oversight, control, integration, and decision-making functions;

▶ Providing capable governance resources to oversee and monitor program uncertainty and complexity related to achieving benefits delivery;

▶ Providing guidance related to organizational strategy;

▶ Ensuring program goals and planned benefits align with organizational strategic and operational goals;

▶ Endorsing or approving program recommendations and changes;

▶ Resolving and remediating escalated program issues and risks;

▶ Providing oversight and monitoring so program benefits are planned, measured, and achieved;

▶ Providing leadership in making, enforcing, carrying out, and communicating decisions;

▶ Defining key messages that are to be communicated to stakeholders and ensuring they are consistent and transparent;

▶ Reviewing expected benefits and benefits delivery; and

▶ Approving program closure or termination.

In small organizations, a single senior executive may assume the responsibilities of a program oversight committee.

Establishing a single committee that maintains—and is accountable for—all critical elements of program oversight within an organization is considered to be the most efficient means for providing effective and adaptive governance oversight. However, under certain circumstances, some programs may need to report to multiple program steering committees. These programs may include those that are sponsored and overseen jointly by private and governmental organizations, programs managed as collaborations among private but otherwise competitive organizations, or programs in exceedingly complex environments whose subject matter experts cannot be effectively assembled into a single program steering committee. When managing programs with these circumstances, it is critical that the systems and methods for the governance framework and the authority for program decision-making be clearly established in the program governance plan.

3.6.2.3 Program Management Office

The program management office facilitates the governance practices. It is a management structure that standardizes the program-related governance processes and facilitates the sharing of resources, methodologies, tools, and techniques. The program management office also provides professional expertise using staff highly trained in applying governance framework practices to provide oversight, support, and decision-making capability to the program, and may extend to monitoring compliance with program management practices.

The design and formation of a program management office is tailored to its environment. For example, organizations pursuing exceptionally large, complicated, or complex programs may establish multiple program management offices, each of which may be dedicated solely to the conduct of one or more critical organizational programs. Variances in the program management office may include an enterprise project management office (EPMO), existing at both the performing and customer operating organizations, or the establishment of a strategic enterprise project management office (SEPMO) or transformation office (TO).

Alternatively, organizations pursuing multiple programs often seek to ensure a high level of consistency and professionalism in the management and governance of their programs by creating a program management office as a formal center of excellence in program governance practices that services a portfolio of different programs. For any program, the program management office may be created or may leverage an existing function. Depending on the context of the program, individuals with specific skills, such as change and benefits management specialists, can be allocated to the program management office.

The functions of a program management office may be delegated to an individual manager with an exceptional understanding of program management and governance practices, or directly to the individual program managers responsible for oversight of the organization's programs. (See Section 3.6.2 for more information on the program management office.)

3.6.2.4 Program Manager

The program manager is the person authorized to manage and oversee the program's interactions with the governance framework function, and is granted authority to make decisions on behalf of the program steering committee. For decisions outside of this agreed-upon authority, it is necessary for the program manager to secure authorization from the program steering committee. A number of factors may influence the authority granted to the program team, including the experience of the program manager, the size and complexity of the program and its components, and the degree of coordination required to manage the program within the context of the larger organization.

The program manager ensures that the program goals and objectives remain aligned with the overall strategic objectives of the organization. Typical governance-related responsibilities include:

- ▶ Assessing the governance framework, including organizational structure, policies, and procedures, and, in some cases, establishing the governance framework;

- ▶ Overseeing program conformance to governance policies and processes;

- ▶ Managing program interactions with the program steering committee and sponsors as well as the interdependencies among components within the program;

- ▶ Monitoring and managing program risks, performance, synergies, and communications;

- ▶ Managing program risks and issues and escalating critical risks and issues beyond the program manager's control to the program steering committee;

- ▶ Monitoring and reporting on overall program funding and health;

- ▶ Assessing program outcomes and requesting authorization from the program steering committee to change overall program strategies;

- ▶ Creating, monitoring, and communicating the program management plan and key internal and external dependencies;

- ▶ Managing, monitoring, and tracking overall program benefits realization; and

- ▶ Managing, monitoring, coaching, and mentoring the project managers and other component managers who are directly part of the program.

Program goals are pursued and benefits are delivered by means of the authorization and initiation of components. The authorization of components under the direction of a parent program is conceptually the same as the authorization of the parent program itself by the program steering committee. Thus, programs have a function similar to that of a governance board. Program managers and program teams may become responsible for governance of a component of a program, often referred to as component governance. In this role, program managers are responsible for defining the framework, functions, and processes by which their program's components will be monitored and managed. The degree of autonomy granted to program managers for oversight of their components, and the mechanisms provided by parent programs, differ among organizations and, at times, among programs being managed within a single organization, the program management office, by the sponsor, or as a process stated in the organization's governance documents. While some organizations choose to have components governed by the same governance framework structure described for a parent program, others allow the parent program to assume independent responsibility for governance of program components. Under such circumstances, a program manager may assume responsibility for establishing a governing framework to manage components within the parent program. (See Section 1.6 for more information on the role of the program manager.)

3.6.2.5 Project Manager(s)

In the context of a program, the project manager role generally refers to the person assigned by the performing organization to lead the team that is responsible for achieving the project objectives that are being pursued as a component of the program. In this context, the project manager responsibilities are defined in the *PMBOK® Guide* [1]. These responsibilities include effective planning, performing, and tracking of a program's component project(s), and delivery of the project's outcomes as defined in the respective project charter and the program management plan. In this capacity, the project manager is subject to component governance oversight by the program manager (acting in a role analogous to that of the program steering committee) and to the program team. While the role is not always central to the governance framework, the typical governance-related responsibilities of a project manager include:

- ▶ Managing project interactions with the program manager, program steering committee, and sponsor;
- ▶ Overseeing project conformance to governance policies and processes;

- ▶ Monitoring and managing project performance and communications;

- ▶ Managing project risks and issues and escalating critical risks and issues beyond the project manager's control to the program manager, sponsor, or program steering committees;

- ▶ Managing internal and external dependencies for the project; and

- ▶ Fostering engagement of key stakeholders.

3.6.2.6 Other Stakeholders

Several other stakeholders may have governance-framework-related roles. The portfolio manager may have a role in ensuring that a program is selected, prioritized, and staffed according to the organization's plan for realizing desired benefits.

As the program progresses, representatives of the organization, such as functional representatives and product owners, ensure that the program's direction is aligned to the end customers' potentially evolving requirements.

When the program delivers a capability to the organization, the expected or potential benefits can only be realized when the organization is prepared to integrate the capability into its operations. The operational manager is generally responsible for receiving and integrating the capabilities delivered by other program components for achieving the desired organizational benefits. This integration may initially lead to disruption and, over the long term, a steady state that is different from the previous environment. It is therefore important to the success of the organization and program that the capability is integrated effectively. The operational manager is supported by individual(s) assigned to the role to manage this change. Such individuals can be the sponsor, representative(s) from the receiving business area, program manager, project manager, and, in many cases, a specialist in managing business change. This role has governance implications as it informs and performs the governance practices described in Section 3.6.1. Typically, the individual in this role will be supported by a team from the corresponding business area.

Other governance-associated roles include specialists in certain aspects of the domain, including risk specialists, human capital, buyers, and contracting experts to develop and govern agreements with third-party vendors.

3.6.3 GOVERNANCE FRAMEWORK DESIGN AND IMPLEMENTATION

A governance framework should begin with the identification of governance participants and the establishment of governance practices. The governance framework must comply with local, state, and national laws regarding competition, conflicts of interest, and procurement procedures. There is also a need to define the specific expectations for how governance-related roles are filled and responsibilities discharged. Governance practices may differ depending on the sector or industry that the organization serves. Governance of programs in such diverse fields as national or local government, aerospace and defense, banking and finance, and pharmaceutical development may have remarkably different needs based on the unique political, regulatory, legal, technical, and competitive environments in which they operate. In each case, however, a sponsor organization seeks to implement governance practices that enable the organization to monitor the program's support of the organizational strategy.

Effective governance ensures that strategic alignment is optimized and the program's targeted benefits are delivered as expected. Governance participants also confirm that all stakeholders are appropriately engaged and that appropriate supportive tools and processes are defined and effectively leveraged. Governance practices provide the foundation for ensuring that decisions are made rationally and with appropriate justification, and that the responsibilities and accountabilities are clearly defined and applied. These activities can be accomplished within the policies and standards of the host and partner organizations and are measured to attain compliance.

The design of the governance framework can have a significant influence on the success of the program. In extreme cases, inappropriate governance may create more problems than its absence, as it can engender a false sense of alignment, progress, and success. There are many factors to consider when designing the program governance rules and framework. Common factors to consider when optimizing and tailoring the governance framework include:

▶ **Legislative environment.** Programs that are significantly influenced by changing legislation may benefit from governance designed for direct interaction with the legislative authorities. In other cases, the interaction may be performed by elements of corporate governance on behalf of the program.

▶ **Decision-making hierarchy.** It is critical for decision-making responsibility to be at the level where competence, accountability, and authority reside. There are complexities to this approach. For example, in organizations where employees are not ultimately accountable for their actions or not made to feel accountable for their actions, there is a greater need for controlling practices. In other circumstances, a highly regarded, successful, and experienced program manager and team may be given greater autonomy and decision-making powers than are typically given to program managers. Such autonomy could include a healthy failure culture in which the team can grow and improve based on its decisions, both successful and unsuccessful.

▶ **Optimized governance.** Generally, it makes sense for the size of the governance framework to be optimized and as streamlined as possible, while still able to perform the practices of the domain. This will lead to role clarity, effective and targeted support from the organization, and ultimately, more rapid and effective decision-making, endorsements, and approvals. The governance framework should not duplicate program management activity.

▶ **Alignment with portfolio and organizational governance.** The governance framework can be impacted by the portfolio governance that it supports. The degree to which program governance should align with organizational governance is based on the number, type, and relative importance of the program governance's interactions with corporate groups and governance. Typically, the need for alignment with organizational governance is greatest in the program definition stage as the governance framework and the program itself are being formulated.

▶ **Program delivery.** A program that regularly delivers benefits to the organization may require a different level of governance than a program delivering all or most of the benefits at the end. Regular delivery of benefits potentially requires constant change in the operations of the organization, and the governance to manage this change is critical throughout the life cycle.

▶ **Contracting.** A program being managed and staffed by employees of the receiving organization may require a different level of governance than a program being delivered by an external party when, in such cases, the management of the legal agreement requires a different governance focus.

▶ **Risk of failure.** The greater the perceived risk of program failure, the greater the likelihood the governance team will monitor progress and success more diligently. This monitoring may manifest in a higher frequency of health checks and less decision-making delegation to the program team.

▶ **Strategic importance.** High-value programs critical to the success of the organization, and delivering benefits that need to be completely aligned with the strategy, may require different or more senior participants on the governance team.

- ▶ **Program management office.** In many project- or program-based organizations, a centralized program management office supports the governance of all programs for that organization. In other organizations, program management offices may be formed specifically for a given program.

- ▶ **Program funding structure.** When funding is secured from outside the delivery organization (e.g., from the World Bank)—where the funding organization mandates the governance model as a condition of ongoing funding—there are likely implications on the design of the governance and the skills required.

In addition to these factors, the phase of the life cycle also influences the governance framework, because the relative importance of different governance practices differs as the program progresses. The corresponding design of the governance should align with required practices in a timely manner.

As a result of the factors described in Section 3.6.3, there are many considerations to account for during the optimization of a governance framework. Once the governance framework is designed and implemented, it is important to exercise mechanisms to analyze and assess its effectiveness and continually improve and optimize it.

For a broader discussion of program governance within the context of organizational, portfolio, and project governance, see *Governance of Portfolios, Programs, and Projects: A Practice Guide* [8].

3.6.4 INTERACTIONS WITH PROGRAM MANAGEMENT PRINCIPLES AND OTHER PROGRAM MANAGEMENT PERFORMANCE DOMAINS

The Governance Framework performance domain is the primary mechanism for overseeing a program's implementation, management, and performance. By establishing practices to support the program and outlining defined roles for all of the involved stakeholders, program managers can effectively align with an organization's strategic and operational goals.

The most vital focus of the Governance Framework performance domain is designing a framework in which the lines of authority are clear, the responsibility and accountability of each position defined, and the levels of decision-making structured to enable optimal delivery of the program and its components. This framework enables a dynamic, synergistic network of relationships across products and processes. Thus, the Governance Framework performance domain influences, and is influenced by, the Governance, Change, and Team of Teams program management principles, as well as the Benefits Management, Collaboration, Stakeholder Engagement, and Strategic Alignment performance domains (see Figure 2-1).

3.7 COLLABORATION

The Collaboration performance domain creates synergy across stakeholders, both internal and external, to optimize benefits delivery and realization. Ultimately, the Collaboration performance domain helps the program team achieve the Synergy, Governance, and Team of Teams program management principles by empowering the program leadership and teams to identify areas within the other performance domains that support optimal delivery of benefits and value.

This section includes:

3.7.1 Collaboration Factors Impacting Program Success

3.7.2 Collaboration for Benefits and Value Delivery Planning

3.7.3 Program Components and Activities Collaboration

3.7.4 Interactions with Program Management Principles and Other Program Management Performance Domains

Collaboration fosters the teamwork necessary for a program to accomplish its objectives across components. However, collaboration at the program level is different and more complex than at the project level because making decisions depends on generating the right levels of synergy. This dynamic encompasses and crosses over the project teams and program team-of-teams structure, internal and external partners, providers, and customers—all working together to build a mutually beneficial partnership for optimal performance outcomes.

Program-level collaboration requires managers and teams to adapt and integrate program management performance domains and supporting activities, working within the program team-of-teams structure, in an effort to optimize benefits realization. Furthermore, projects have specific deliverables and outcomes, whereas program value is determined by benefits that might not be delivered or derived at the same time. Thus, planning how benefits realization and organizational value delivery will be achieved over the program's life cycle—and management—requires balancing across components in a collaborative manner.

Collaboration should be evaluated in terms of the capabilities and capacity needed throughout a program's life cycle, the resources that the program needs for sustainment, and the pace at which the program's activities should be coordinated and timed for benefits delivery. A key part of successful collaboration is clear communication across project and program teams and other component teams.

Use of a program-level responsibility assignment matrix (RAM) can assist collaboration efforts across the program components, setting expectations for specific components. Realizing success across these components—whether projects, subsidiary programs, or other program-related activities—requires more than a governance framework or stakeholder engagement. For synergy, a key program management principle, to be reached, collaboration should balance diverse component needs, which at times might be in competition or even conflict with one another. These conflicts might occur because of competing component interdependencies, shifting performances, changing priorities, or differing component stakeholders. First and foremost, program teams should always prioritize strategic alignment across the program's life cycle and prevent any single outcome from becoming the focus.

Collaboration also is intended to effectively manage a program's life cycle if it is part of a larger portfolio and should align supporting activities (see Figure 3-9). Collaboration is the program management performance domain that addresses, through both leadership and management, the adaptability and resiliency needed at the program level to respond to strategic changes in the overall organizational and portfolio contexts.

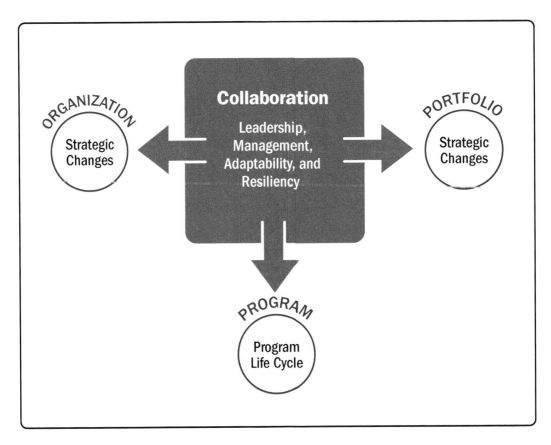

Figure: 3-9. Collaboration at the Program Level

3.7.1 COLLABORATION FACTORS IMPACTING PROGRAM SUCCESS

Several factors influence the success of collaboration. While these factors are not distinctly applicable to programs alone, they will be tailored differently when managing programs versus portfolios or projects. Managing these factors is essential to collaboration efforts and supporting a balanced program that delivers on its intended benefits and outcomes.

3.7.1.1 Engagement

Engagement is one of the most important factors affecting the success of any collaborative process. The program management principles of Team of Teams and Stakeholders are the key drivers for engagement. Collaboration requires an understanding of goals, objectives, and expectations, as well as mutual agreement on the outcomes of the collaborative process among stakeholders and partners. This collaborative process is only possible if everyone who needs to participate is engaged properly. Engagement allows the program management principles to be exercised through the collaborative approach. The consequences of not effectively engaging a key stakeholder may be disinterest, ambiguity regarding expectations, confusion regarding expected outcomes, and failure to deliver. Project-level engagement is driven by the project charter, project planning and contracts, stakeholder engagement, and successfully completing the project's deliverables. Portfolio-level engagement focuses on strategic alignment for portfolio or organizational value achievement. In contrast, program-level engagement requires engaging with stakeholders and partners, focusing on benefits delivery and the needs of program components and operations. Communication is the primary tool for engagement that should be effectively applied to make collaboration work. Communication is essential to understanding complexities, resolving challenges, clarifying ambiguities, effectively mitigating threats, and capitalizing on opportunities.

3.7.1.2 Alignment

Alignment is essential to, and one of the main reasons for, collaboration. The program management principles of Change, Synergy, and Benefits Realization support the program's alignment with organizational strategy. Alignment means understanding and agreeing on some aspect or expectation between two collaborating parties. In the case of program management, alignment is multidirectional and applies to several areas:

▶ Strategic alignment between the program and its portfolio or the organization;

▶ Benefits and outcomes alignment among the program and its constituent projects, components, and activities;

▶ Deliverables and outcomes alignment among the program's partners;

▶ Alignment of expected rewards among the program's sponsors, champions, and organizational leadership;

▶ Alignment of compliance between the governance bodies and the program;

▶ Alignment between the program and the organizational risk appetite; and

▶ Alignment between team and program resources.

3.7.1.3 Complexity

One of the key outcomes of collaboration is addressing the complexities of program execution. Project-level complexities are typically resolved through scope management, progressive elaboration, and change management. Portfolio-level complexities are dealt with more reactively by continuously balancing the portfolio. In the case of programs, certain complexities will be known up front when the program is initiated and respective stakeholders and partners first collaborate. Other complexities will arise over the course of the program life cycle from any internal or external area of program execution: procedure, capacity, communication, governance, behavior, strategy, or change. Regardless, complexities lead to uncertainties and can threaten the program's objectives. Resolving most uncertainties requires collaboration, which should feed into the risk management process of the program and support the proper translation of uncertainties into risks for mitigation or capitalization. The program management principles of Synergy, Risk, and Change are closely tied to managing program complexities effectively. Collaboration requires handling or mitigating risks. This collaboration process involves exploring synergies among collaborating parties to capitalize on opportunities, or monitoring ambiguities and challenges and taking steps to reduce complexities. While project risk focuses on minimizing threats and maximizing opportunities, and portfolio risk focuses on balancing threats and opportunities, program risk lies between the two because collaboration requires analyzing and assessing the kind of risk response needed. Complexities can become threats that silently erode the effectiveness of collaboration. Complexities can also signal an opportunity that one could exploit or enhance to enable more productive collaboration.

For a broader discussion of complexity within the context of organizational, portfolio, and project governance, see *The Standard for Risk Management in Portfolios, Programs, and Projects* [6].

3.7.1.4 Transparency

Transparency enables traceability in the collaborative process. Project-level transparency can largely be achieved through proper reporting and communication. However, collaboration on more complex initiatives, such as portfolios and programs, may be affected by unintentional or intentional concealment of information. This is why the program management principles of Stakeholders, Leadership, and Governance are key drivers of transparency for effective collaboration on programs. The absence of proper collaboration with leadership or stakeholders can create ambiguity and confusion, cause mistrust, and erode transparency for a program. Proper transparency prevents aspects of program execution and the collaborative process from being hidden and is a function and objective of governance. Hence, proper compliance with the governance framework will ensure that collaborative efforts have the proper levels of transparency, which is enabled through proper communication and reporting as well as open decision-making. One of the primary effects of a lack of transparency during any collaborative exercise is the erosion of trust between the parties. Without the requisite levels of trust, any collaboration is susceptible to failure.

The program/project management information systems have an essential role in supporting the value of transparency among the stakeholders.

3.7.1.5 Consultation

An important factor that is essential to effective collaboration is consultation. Consultation is driven by the program management principles of Leadership and Stakeholders. Because collaboration requires information exchange among multiple parties, it is important to access program stakeholders and partners for the right information when needed. Consultation has a direct impact on the timing of the collaborative process because it directly impacts the decision-making process. The right decisions should be made at the right times, which is only possible when the right parties are consulted for the right information at the right times. This also requires the program manager and the program management function to facilitate and coordinate the consultation process by removing barriers and obstacles; communicating effectively; and ensuring information flows accurately, clearly, and efficiently between the requisite producers and consumers of that information. The effectiveness of consultation is also an area impacted by the overall organizational culture in which the program exists. Consultations will be reactive and procedural if the culture is not transparent and results- and goal-oriented. For the program's external environment, it is also important to have the requisite level of consultations with the governance team or function.

3.7.1.6 Culture

The organizational culture is the single most important factor influencing the effectiveness of the collaborative process. Collaboration works in a change-oriented culture. The program management principles of Leadership, Change, and Risk are key drivers for the cultural aspect of collaboration. Leadership sets the tone and ground rules of the culture in which the program exists. If an organization has information silos, a lack of transparency, resistance to trust-based communication, or a culture of withholding emerging information and only releasing it in response to bureaucratic procedures and authoritarian norms or personal influences, then collaboration will be merely ceremonial and procedural. The effects of culture on program components and projects may have less impact because they are more procedurally managed and process driven. Culture will have a stronger effect at the portfolio and program levels. The effectiveness of collaboration may become anchored in the personalities and influences of the program manager, key stakeholders, or partners associated with the program. Representation in the collaborative process may be dependent upon influence and power, rather than participation and empowerment for the success of organizational change. Creating a positive, change-oriented culture ripe for collaboration requires the support and participation of everyone in the organization, from top leadership to task workers.

3.7.1.7 Empathy

Program managers should also leverage the collaborative process to create support for the program. The program management principles of Stakeholders and Leadership are key drivers for creating empathy when collaborating. An important factor beyond the rigid execution of a program is the perception regarding its importance and usefulness. Programs can—and do—become derailed, misunderstood, or even terminated prematurely based on their developing perceptions, which may not match reality. Therefore, collaboration goes beyond procedures, processes, and people in the form of perceptions of value. Beyond the mechanical or systematic execution of a program, the collaborative process should also promote and emphasize empathy for the program's goals, benefits, and outcomes. This aspect is directly related to the morale and interest of the participants. If the program stakeholders and collaborating partners do not perceive the value of the program, think the program (in whole or some part of it) is a waste of their time, feel they are being forced to participate, or are only robotically carrying out their duties, the impact may range from lackadaisical attitudes to active avoidance and a lack of focus on delivering the goals and objectives. This, in turn, will affect the program's performance and ability to meet its benefits realization goals and planned outcomes. For collaboration to be successful, the program manager should track how parties feel about the program and nurture the perception of its value to the organization.

3.7.2 COLLABORATION FOR BENEFITS AND VALUE DELIVERY PLANNING

A program's primary objective is providing cumulative value in the form of benefits (see Section 3.4). In the context of a program, the program's value is defined as all of the quantifiable and qualifiable benefits and the total sum of all tangible and intangible elements derived from the program. This value delivery stems from thorough planning, strategic alignment, and focused directives at the organizational or portfolio levels. A system for value delivery is closely tied to the program's life cycle, and value delivery is realized through a series of outcomes. This value delivery might not be in the form of benefits alone. Overall capacity and capability of the program team, its intangible worth to the organization, and the expected outcome potential during the program's life cycle are critical factors in the value delivery equation.

At the organizational and portfolio levels, planning occurs in response to strategic goals driven by the organization's purpose, vision, and mission. Figure 3-10 illustrates how organizational strategy at the portfolio level drives collaboration. These goals set the value expectations for the organization's programs and translate into sets of specific benefits to be derived from the programs.

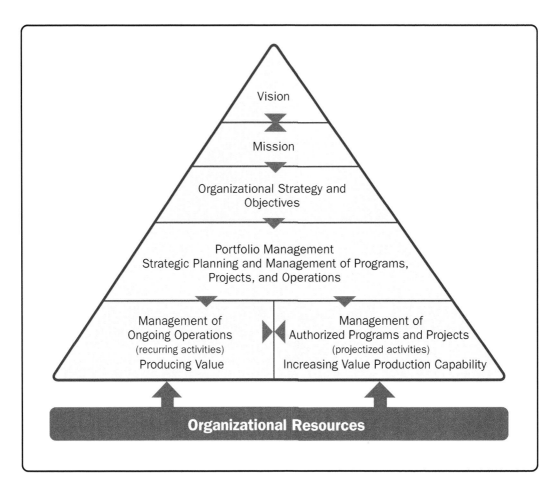

Figure 3-10. The Organizational Context of Portfolio Management and Its Role in Fostering a Culture of Collaboration

Goals, targets, and expectations of value at the organization and portfolio levels should be distilled into program value elements and specific measurable outcomes for program benefits to be effectively planned and realized. This is achieved through the Benefits Management performance domain (see Section 3.4), which defines and prioritizes program components and their interdependencies. A collaboration plan that optimizes value should also be part of the process, as synergies should be captured across the program components.

Drivers of value for programs may include both tangible and intangible benefits. During planning, program managers should clearly understand how collaboration can increase benefits and improve organizational value. This grasp of each benefit, along with a constructive collaboration plan, will enable the program manager to effectively tailor management principles for the successful delivery of benefits.

The execution of program-level planning can only be successful through collaboration across the program management performance domains. This collaboration starts with understanding the program's organizational capacity and capability, which may be managed at the portfolio level. Shortfalls may need to be filled through collaboration with internal and external organizations, which also entails resolving conflicts and balancing the program among expectations, benefits, and continuously evolving challenges, including constraints, assumptions, issues, risks, and opportunities. These expectations and challenges form the foundation of the program management plan development within the Life Cycle Management performance domain (see Section 3.8).

As with all types of change management, program planning is not a one-time, singular exercise. It is subject to the change management process itself, so plans for managing the program are adjusted in response to changes in benefits expectations and realization. Thus, the collaboration planning will also need to evolve.

Understanding dependencies and examining possible synergies up front during planning allows the program to be proactively balanced. Reactive program balancing may become synonymous with, or devolve into, damage control if the program is attempting to capture missed opportunities or deflect challenges derailing the balance and pace of the program. Proactively balancing a program involves managing its pace, whereas benefits planning and realization align with overarching strategy and expectations in a manner that can be achieved across components, given the maturity of collaboration.

At the program level, the program manager should understand and facilitate the planning of underlying projects and program components by controlling the level of collaboration among teams and stakeholders at required levels. Collaboration at the program level requires working with various teams across the value chain in a lean manner and supporting their plans, so they can adapt to program needs.

Governance plays a vital role in planning because such structures lay the framework for how the program may be planned and updated, as synergies are sought to rebalance the program. As the program is continuously balanced, the program manager should collaborate across the governance structure to ensure the program's strategic alignment and value delivery are achievable.

3.7.3 PROGRAM COMPONENTS AND ACTIVITIES COLLABORATION

The benefits and outcomes expected from the program should align with the organization and portfolio expectations and plans. The result is a collaboration chain, from the organizational goals down to the deliverables and outcomes, which is achieved through a dynamic collaboration process that considers the vision, mission, strategy, benefits, and outcomes—as well as the corresponding capabilities, capacity, resources, pace, and partnerships—needed for the program and its components to succeed.

The success of project- and component-level collaboration relies upon the working relationships among subsidiary programs; program activities; project, operations, and component managers; teams and their respective stakeholders; and effective communication among them. Project-level collaboration requires a proper business and systems analysis to be done, according to the principle of progressive elaboration of requirements, followed by effective change control to manage scope or requirements baselines.

Program managers need to effectively oversee this process, with proper leadership through the Governance Framework performance domain, to support the scope management processes, communications, and conflict resolution. However, program managers also have visibility into the benefits to be realized from various program components, which the program components may not, and thus should make sure collaboration supports the overall demands and goals of program benefits.

The elements within a program, including subsidiary programs, projects, and components, often strive to achieve their individual successes through their own life cycle processes, and do not necessarily consider the higher-level benefits and goals of the program.

Conflict in which the needs of the program components are not aligned with those of the overall program could create a scenario where a component's efforts to minimize its own challenges may, in certain situations, increase the program's overall challenges or cause potential failure. The program manager is responsible for balancing the individual demands and goals of the respective components against the overall demands of the program. The program manager's objective is to ensure the program succeeds, even if specific components do not.

The balancing aspect of collaboration emphasizes that, even though proper scope management, communications management, stakeholder engagement, and governance procedures are all being followed, the program should be balanced with respect to the program's overall benefits realization pace and value schedule.

Program components may follow their own distinct or tailored approaches for execution. These approaches, such as specific agile or lean approaches, are typically intended to improve the overall effectiveness and efficiency for each project or component execution, as defined for each component. The program management function should also ensure that isolated optimization or execution of efficiency initiatives by program components and activities do not result in challenges for other program components or an imbalance in program benefits realization goals. This can happen if the timing of benefits realization is affected because of different levels of efficiency and pace across program components. Outside factors, such as capabilities and resource capacity, also influence the pace of different program components and activities. Balancing the program requires facilitating collaboration among program components and activities, so they understand how their individual paces affect the overall program goals and objectives.

3.7.4 INTERACTIONS WITH PROGRAM MANAGEMENT PRINCIPLES AND OTHER PROGRAM MANAGEMENT PERFORMANCE DOMAINS

The Collaboration performance domain stresses key interpersonal skills such as empathy, constructive communication, and proactive engagement, as well as vital corporate practices like transparency, risk, and building trust and respect. The concept of collaboration is woven into all elements of a program, regardless of focus area or stakeholder specialties or expertise. Integrating a diversity of ideas, perspectives, and experiences enables discussions, problem-solving, decision-making, and greater rewards for participants in the process.

Furthermore, strong partnerships are the backbone of constructive communication, interweaving mutual agreement on the benefits of various program practices; an understanding of goals, objectives, and expectations; and a desire to realize program benefits—today and in the future. This interconnectedness of ideas and priorities demonstrates how the collaboration network aligns with the Synergy, Governance, and Team of Teams program management principles, and the Benefits Management, Stakeholder Engagement, Governance Framework, Strategic Alignment, and Life Cycle Management performance domains (see Figure 3-1).

3.8 LIFE CYCLE MANAGEMENT

Life Cycle Management is the program management performance domain that manages the program life cycle and the phases required to facilitate effective program definition, delivery, and closure.

This section includes:

3.8.1 Program Definition Phase

3.8.2 Program Delivery Phase

3.8.3 Program Closure Phase

3.8.4 Interactions with Program Management Principles and Other Program Management Performance Domains

In order to ensure the realization of benefits, programs provide the necessary alignment of the organization's strategic goals and objectives with the individual components. These components may include projects, subsidiary programs, and additional program-related phases that are necessary to achieve the specified goals and objectives. Since programs, by nature, involve a certain level of uncertainty, change, complexity, and interdependency among the various components, it is useful to establish a common and consistent set of processes that can be applied across phases. These discrete phases, which may sometimes overlap, constitute the program life cycle. The Life Cycle Management performance domain spans the duration of the program, during which it contributes to, and integrates with, the other program management performance domains as well as the supporting program phases.

Programs function similarly to projects in that the program is defined, benefits are delivered, and the program is closed. Unlike projects, however, programs involve the coordination and sequencing of multiple components above what is required at an individual project level. The phases executed within the program life cycle are dependent on the specific type of program and typically begin before funding is approved or when the program manager is assigned. There is often considerable effort expended prior to defining and approving a program. (See Sections 3.3 and 3.6 for more information about strategic alignment and the governance framework.)

During program delivery, components are authorized, planned, and executed, and benefits are delivered. In some cases, though, there are benefits that will be achieved after the program closure, not just in the delivery phase.

Program closure is then approved by the program steering committee when the desired benefits or program objectives have been realized or the steering committee has determined that the program should be terminated. Reasons for early termination may be a change in organizational strategy with which the program is no longer aligned or an assessment that the planned benefits may no longer be achievable.

Programs often span long durations—multiple years and, in some cases, decades. Regardless of duration, all programs follow a similar trajectory.

To achieve the organization's optimum value and benefits, programs are implemented using three major phases, which include:

▶ **Program definition phase.** Program definition consists of program phases conducted to authorize the program and develop the program management plan required to achieve the expected results. As part of program definition, the program business case, program charter, and program roadmap are formulated. Once approved, the program management plan is prepared.

▶ **Program delivery phase.** Program delivery comprises the program phases performed to produce the intended results of each component in accordance with the program management plan. Throughout this phase, individual components are initiated, planned, executed, monitored, controlled, evaluated, and closed, while benefits are delivered, transitioned, and sustained.

▶ **Program closure phase.** This phase technically closes the program by archiving the documents, transferring the lessons learned to organizational process assets (OPAs), refunding the remaining budget, disposing of the resources, and transferring the remaining risk to the organization. During this closure, work is transitioned to operations.

Figure 3-11 shows the phases that compose the program life cycle. These phases are further explained in Sections 3.8.1 through 3.8.3.

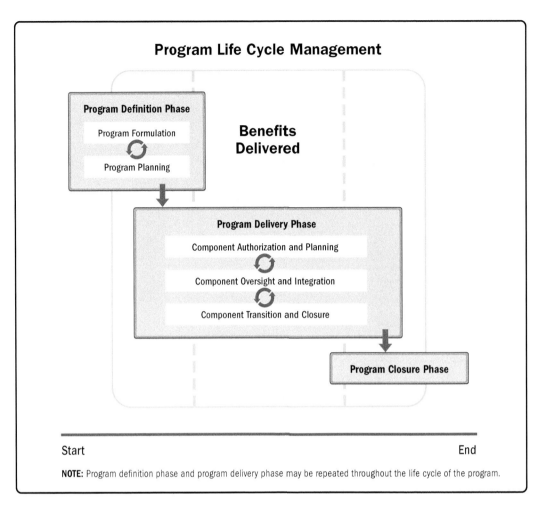

Figure 3-11. Program Life Cycle Phases

The Standard for Program Management

3.8.1 PROGRAM DEFINITION PHASE

The program definition phase includes program phases conducted to authorize the program and develop the program management plan required to achieve the expected results; it typically includes phases that are performed as the result of an organization's business case to fulfill strategic objectives or achieve a desired state within an organization's portfolio. There may be a number of phases executed by a portfolio management body prior to the start of the program definition phase. The portfolio management body develops concepts (e.g., products, services, organizational outcomes), scope frameworks, initial requirements, timelines, deliverables, and acceptable cost guidelines.

The primary purpose of the program definition phase is to progressively elaborate the goals and objectives to be addressed by the program, define the expected program benefits and outcomes, and seek approval for the program. Program definition should fall into two distinct but overlapping subphases: program formulation and program planning. The program manager is selected and assigned during program formulation.

3.8.1.1 Program Formulation

Program formulation involves the development of the program business case that states the overall expected benefits to be addressed by the program in support of the strategic initiatives. During this subphase, the sponsoring organization also assigns a program sponsor to oversee and govern the program. The sponsor's key responsibilities include securing financing for the program and selecting the program manager responsible for conducting and managing the program. The assignment of the program manager and the definition of their roles, responsibilities, and organizational interfaces should be done as early as possible, as this individual effectively guides the program formulation phase and facilitates the development of the required outcomes. To demonstrate how the program can deliver the desired organizational benefits, the sponsor, sponsoring organization, and program manager work closely together to:

▸ Initiate studies and estimates of scope, resources, and cost;

▸ Develop an initial risk assessment and other high-level assessment (scope, finance, schedule, resource, change, quality, communication, procurement, information); and

▸ Develop a program charter and program management plan with milestones.

Studies of scope, resources, and cost are also performed to assess the organization's ability to deliver the program. At this time, the proposed program is compared with other organizational initiatives to determine the priority of the program under consideration. This information serves as an important input into the creation of the business case if it was not developed by the portfolio management body. If the business case was developed prior to program formulation, it is revised and updated accordingly. Additionally, an initial risk assessment is conducted to analyze threats and opportunities. This analysis helps determine the probability of the program's successful delivery of organizational benefits and identify risk response strategies and plans. (See Section 4.3.11 for additional information on program risk.)

The program charter serves as the primary document to decide if the program will be authorized, and is reviewed by the portfolio management body when within a portfolio structure or suitable governing body for stand-alone programs. Approval of the charter formally authorizes the commencement of the program, provides the program manager with the authority to apply organizational resources to program phases, and connects the program to the organization's ongoing work and strategic priorities. If the program is not authorized, this information should be recorded, and the documentation should be appropriately archived and captured in a lessons learned repository.

The outcomes of program formulation may continue to be updated throughout the program definition phase as business results are measured and the planned outcomes become more defined.

3.8.1.2 Program Planning

Program planning commences upon formal approval of the program charter by the program sponsor. In this phase, a governance structure is established, the initial program organization is defined, and a team is assembled to develop the program management plan. The program management plan is a document that integrates the program's subsidiary plans and establishes the management controls and overall plan for integrating and managing the program's individual components. These controls measure performance against the program management plan using information collected and consolidated from the constituent projects. Its main purpose is to enable the program to be continually aligned with the strategic priorities of the organization in order to deliver the expected benefits. The program management plan is developed based on the organization's strategic plan, business case, program charter, and any other outcomes as they emerge during the program formulation.

This plan is the key outcome created during program planning and may be combined into one plan or multiple plans that include the following subsidiary documents:

- ▶ Benefits management plan (see Section 3.4),
- ▶ Stakeholder engagement plan (see Section 3.5),
- ▶ Governance plan (see Section 3.6),
- ▶ Change management plan (see Section 4.3.4),
- ▶ Communications management plan (see Section 4.3.5),
- ▶ Financial management plan (see Section 4.3.6),
- ▶ Information management plan (see Section 4.3.7),
- ▶ Procurement management plan (see Section 4.3.8),
- ▶ Quality management plan (see Section 4.3.9),
- ▶ Resource management plan (see Section 4.3.10),
- ▶ Risk management plan (see Section 4.3.11),
- ▶ Schedule management plan (see Section 4.3.12), and
- ▶ Scope management plan (see Section 4.3.13).

Once the program management plan has been approved, the program delivery phase can begin. It is important to remember, regardless of whether using adaptive or predictive planning techniques, that this plan will be iterated and constraints may arise due to changes in critical factors such as business goals, deliverables, benefits, time, and cost. To address these factors, updates and revisions to the program management plan, its roadmap, and its subsidiary plans are approved or rejected through the program steering committee, which will reflect the planning techniques the program is using.

The program delivery phase begins after the program management plan is reviewed and formally approved.

3.8.2 PROGRAM DELIVERY PHASE

The program delivery phase includes program phases performed to produce the intended results of each component in accordance with the program management plan. This phase is considered iterative instead of linear, as the capabilities produced by each component are integrated into the overall program to facilitate delivery of the intended program benefits. The program management team provides oversight and support to position the components for successful completion. Component work and phases are integrated under the program umbrella to facilitate the management and delivery of program benefits. The work in this phase includes the program and execution of the program components. Component management plans (covering cost management, scope management, schedule management, risk management, resource management, etc.) are developed at the component level (component-level work) and integrated at the program level (integrative work) to maintain alignment with the program direction to deliver the program benefits. Interactions with components to accomplish goals, manage changes, and address risks and issues are managed throughout the program in order to position the program for success.

Programs often have a significant level of uncertainty. While the program management plan may document the intended direction and benefits of the program, the full suite of program components may not be known; there might not even be a desire for them to be known. To accommodate this uncertainty, the program manager needs to use the concept of progressive elaboration to allow for adaptations as the program is executed. The program manager is also responsible for managing this group of components in a consistent, coordinated way in order to achieve results that could not be obtained by managing the components as stand-alone efforts. Each program component will progress through the following program delivery subphases:

▶ Component authorization and planning,

▶ Component oversight and integration, and

▶ Component transition and closure.

Program delivery ends when the program governance determines that the specific criteria for this phase have been satisfied or a decision is made to terminate the program.

The Standard for Program Management

3.8.2.1 Component Authorization and Planning

Component authorization involves the initiation of components based on the organization's specified criteria and individual business cases developed for each component. These criteria are generally included in the program governance plan. The Governance Framework performance domain provides guidance for processes leading to component authorization. A number of phases are required to verify that a component properly supports the program's outcomes and aligns with the strategy and ongoing work of the organization prior to authorization. These phases may include performing a needs analysis, conducting a feasibility study, or creating a plan to ensure the projects realize their intended benefits. (See Section 3.6 for more information on the governance framework.)

Component planning is performed throughout the duration of the program delivery phase in response to events that require significant replanning or new component initiation requests (submitted by the requesting component). Component planning includes the phases needed to integrate the component into the program to position each component for successful execution. These phases involve formalizing the scope of the work to be accomplished by the component and identifying the deliverables that will satisfy the program's goals and benefits.

Each component may have associated management plans. These associated management plans can include a project management plan or component plan, transition plan, operations plan, maintenance plan, or other type of plan, depending upon the type of work under consideration. The appropriate information from each component plan is integrated into the associated program management plan. This plan includes information used by the program to help manage and oversee the overall program's progress.

3.8.2.2 Component Oversight and Integration

In the context of a program, some components may produce benefits individually, while some components should be integrated with others before the associated benefits may be realized. Each component team executes its associated plans and program integrative work. Throughout this activity, component teams provide status and other information to the program manager and their associated components, so their efforts may be integrated into, and coordinated with, the overall program phases. There might be cases where the program manager may initiate a new component to consolidate the integration efforts of multiple components. Without this step, individual components may produce deliverables; the benefits, however, may not be realized without the coordinated delivery.

3.8.2.3 Component Transition and Closure

After the program components have produced deliverables and coordinated the successful delivery of their products, services, or results, these components are typically scheduled for closure or transition to operations or ongoing work. Component transition addresses the need for ongoing phases, such as product support, service management, change management, user engagement, or customer support from a program component to an operational support function, in order for the ongoing benefits to be achieved. The criteria for performing these phases, as well as the organizational expectations, are documented in the governance plan.

Prior to the end of the program delivery phase, all component areas are reviewed to verify the benefits were delivered and to transition any remaining projects and sustaining phases. The final status is reviewed with the program sponsor and program steering committee before authorizing formal program closure.

3.8.3 PROGRAM CLOSURE PHASE

The program closure phase includes the program phases necessary to transition program benefits to the sustaining organization and formally close the program. During program transition, the program steering committee is consulted to determine whether: (a) the program has met all of the desired benefits and that all transition work has been performed within the component transition, or (b) there is another program or sustaining activity that will oversee the ongoing benefits for which this program was chartered. In the second instance, there may be work required to transition the resources, responsibilities, risks, knowledge, good practices, and lessons learned to another sustaining entity. Once the transitioning phases are completed, the program manager receives approval from the portfolio management body to formally close the program. During this closure phase, specific activities are performed, which are described in detail in Section 4.4.

3.8.4 INTERACTIONS WITH PROGRAM MANAGEMENT PRINCIPLES AND OTHER PROGRAM MANAGEMENT PERFORMANCE DOMAINS

Each program is unique, with its own distinct mission and life cycle. From conception to planning, delivery to long-term sustainment, or even closure, programs are shaped by the expertise and experiences of their management teams and associated stakeholders. These individuals usually come from a variety of corporate domains, creating a need for strong communication and teamwork. If they do their jobs right, everyone involved can establish a productive, long-lasting program providing abundant benefits to the organization.

The Life Cycle Management performance domain requires program and project managers to optimize their leadership and oversight skills, while balancing program structure, requirements, and the needs of various stakeholders. The ultimate goal is to effectively monitor the program's creation, evolution, and benefits gained by the organization. In this respect, the Life Cycle Management performance domain exemplifies the Benefits Realization, Synergy, and Governance program management principles, as well as the Benefits Management, Collaboration, Governance Framework, Stakeholder Engagement, and Strategic Alignment performance domains (see Figure 2-1).

Program Activities

Program activities are tasks conducted to support a program throughout its life cycle. This section includes:

4.1 Program Integration Management

4.2 Program Definition Phase Activities

4.3 Program Delivery Phase Activities

4.4 Program Closure Phase Activities

All work performed in a program for the purpose of overall program management is collectively known as *program activities*. Typically, program activities are interdependent and complementary, since the deliverables produced from one particular activity may be necessary to perform another activity. The names and descriptions of these activities may appear to be similar to those of project activities or processes; however, their content, scope, and complexity are different. For example, project risk management activities focus on risks to project execution and success, whereas program risk management incorporates escalated project and program risks while also monitoring interdependencies that affect multiple component projects.

The processes, tools, methods, and artifacts used in project-level activities can be found in the *PMBOK® Guide* [1] and *Process Groups: A Practice Guide* [2]. The corresponding program activities encompass a greater number of inputs and typically broader scope. For example, results of the individual component's project risk planning efforts provide input to the program risk planning effort. Risk control is performed continuously at both the component level and the program level; project-level risks may be escalated to the program level or may have a cumulative effect that requires the risks to be addressed at the program level.

It is important to note that program activities directly support the individual components to enable the component activities to help achieve the program objectives. The deliverables created at the project level that directly contribute to the program benefits and milestones achieved are monitored at the program level by the program manager to provide consistency with the overall program strategy. Management of component-level activities is still handled by the project manager.

Given the scope and complexity of a program, numerous supporting program activities are performed throughout the program life cycle. The definitions and terminology associated with these activities at the program level are very similar to those at the project level. However, program activities operate at a higher level, dealing with multiple projects, subsidiary programs, and other programs, and address links between the program and organizational strategy. While programs may utilize component-level information, the activities should integrate the information to reflect a program perspective.

The program activities that support program management and governance include:

- ▶ Program integration management,
- ▶ Program change management,
- ▶ Program communications management,
- ▶ Program financial management,
- ▶ Program information management,
- ▶ Program procurement management,
- ▶ Program quality management,
- ▶ Program resource management,
- ▶ Program risk management,
- ▶ Program schedule management, and
- ▶ Program scope management.

The program activities enable a strategic approach to planning, managing, and delivering program outputs and benefits. Program-management-supporting activities require coordination with functional groups in the organization, but in a broader context than similar activities supporting a single project. The extent to which each activity can be completed, and the formality of outcomes, will depend on the size of the program, industry, organizational standards, and life cycle. Programs using iterative and incremental life cycles might have fewer formal activities and less formal outputs.

4.1 PROGRAM INTEGRATION MANAGEMENT

As defined in Section 1, program management refers to the alignment of various components, such as projects, subsidiary programs, and program activities, to achieve the planned program goals and benefits. The practices applied during this process are used to optimize or integrate the costs, schedules, and efforts of the individual components to manage and deliver maximum benefits at the program level instead of the component level.

Program activities and integration management are concerned with collectively utilizing the resources, knowledge, and skills available to deploy multiple components throughout the program life cycle. This process also involves making decisions regarding:

▶ Competing demands and priorities,

▶ Threats and opportunities,

▶ Resource allocations,

▶ Changes due to uncertainty and complexity of the program scope,

▶ Interdependencies among components, and

▶ Coordination of work to meet the program objectives.

Program activities and integration management are more cyclical and iterative in nature, as adjustments may be required based on the actual benefits and outcomes produced to realign the program with the strategic priorities.

4.1.1 PROGRAM INTEGRATION MANAGEMENT ACTIVITIES

Program integration management is the core activity that occurs across the entire program life cycle. It includes the activities needed to identify, define, combine, unify, and coordinate multiple components into the program. Throughout the program integration activities, there are numerous interactions with other program management performance domains (see Section 2). This section focuses on the following activities and when they are performed throughout the program life cycle phases:

- ▶ Program infrastructure development (see Section 4.1),
- ▶ Program delivery management (see Section 4.3.1),
- ▶ Program performance management (see Section 4.3.2),
- ▶ Benefits management activity (see Section 4.3.3), and
- ▶ Program change sustainment plan (see Section 4.4.1).

4.1.2 MAPPING OF THE PROGRAM LIFE CYCLE TO PROGRAM ACTIVITIES

Table 4-1 maps the program management life cycle's three major phases to the program-supporting activities. Although these supporting activities occur throughout the program life cycle, each activity is mapped to where most of the work takes place. Informal preplanning exercises may take place in earlier phases for each consideration.

Table 4-1. Mapping of Program Management Life Cycle Phases to Core and Supporting Activities

Core and Supporting Program Activities	Program Life Cycle Phases			
	Program Definition		Program Delivery	Program Closure
	Program Formulation	Program Planning		
Program Integration Management	Program Infrastructure Development Program Performance Management	Program Management Planning Program Performance Management	Program Delivery Management Program Performance Management Benefits Sustainment and Program Transition	Program Closeout Program Performance Management
Program Change Management	Program Change Assessment	Program Change Management Planning	Program Change Management	Benefits Transition Planning
Program Communications Management	Program Communications Assessment	Program Communications Management Planning	Program Communications Management Program Information Distribution Method Program Reporting Benefits Updates	
Program Financial Management	Program Initial Cost Estimation	Program Cost Estimation Program Financial Framework Establishment Program Financial Management Planning	Program Financial Management Program Cost Budgeting Component Cost Estimation	Program Financial Closure
Program Information Management	Program Information Management Assessment	Program Information Management Planning	Program Information Management	Program Information Archiving and Transition
Program Procurement Management	Program Procurement Assessment	Program Procurement Management Planning	Program Procurement Management Program Contract Administration	Program Procurement Closure
Program Quality Management	Program Quality Assessment	Program Quality Management Planning	Program Quality Assurance and Control Program Quality Control	
Program Resource Management	Program Resource Requirements Estimation	Program Resource Management Planning	Program Resource Management Resource Interdependency Management	Program Resource Transition
Program Risk Management	Program Initial Risk Assessment	Program Risk Management Planning Program Risk Identification	Program Risk Management Program Risk Identification Program Risk Analysis Program Risk Response Management	Program Risk Transition
Program Schedule Management	Program Schedule Assessment Benefits Milestones	Program Schedule Management Planning	Program Schedule Management	
Program Scope Management	Program Scope Assessment	Program Scope Management Planning	Program Scope Management	

4.2 PROGRAM DEFINITION PHASE ACTIVITIES

The program definition phase establishes and confirms the business case for the program and then develops the detailed plan for its delivery. This phase is divided into two parts: program formulation and program planning.

4.2.1 PROGRAM FORMULATION ACTIVITIES

In program formulation, the high-level scope, risks, costs, and expected benefits of the program are assessed to confirm that the program provides a viable way forward for the organization and is strategically aligned with the organization's objectives. Program activities supporting program formulation are often exploratory in nature, looking at a number of possible alternatives to help ensure the ones best aligned with strategy and organizational preferences can be identified and approved for inclusion in the program. In some cases, however, the program formulation activities conclude that the program does not have a strong business case and should be canceled.

Figure 4-1 illustrates how program formulation activities contribute to the development of the program business case and program charter through the core activity of program integration management.

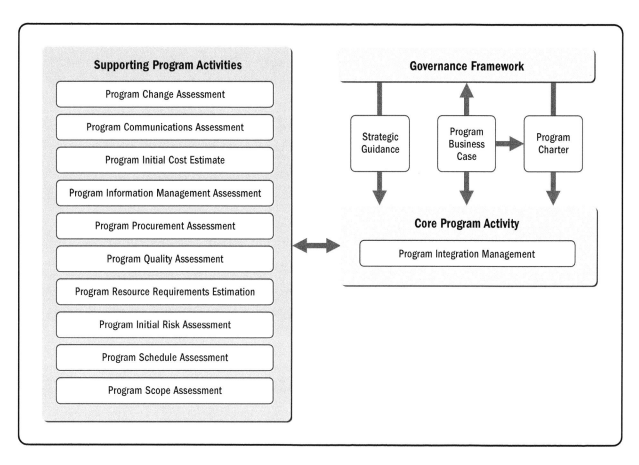

Figure 4-1. Program Formulation Phase Activity Interaction

4.2.2 PROGRAM PLANNING PHASE ACTIVITIES

In program planning, the program organization is defined and an initial team is deployed to develop the program management plan. The program management plan is developed based on the organization's strategic plan, business case, program charter, and the outcomes of the assessments completed during program definition. The plan includes the roadmap of the program components and the management arrangements through which program delivery should be overseen. The plan should be open for changes, taking into consideration that the success of a program is not measured against its baseline but by how an organization is able to realize benefits from the program outcomes. The program management plan is therefore a reference document and should be viewed as a managed baseline.

Figure 4-2 illustrates how program planning activities support development of the program management plan through the core activity of program integration management.

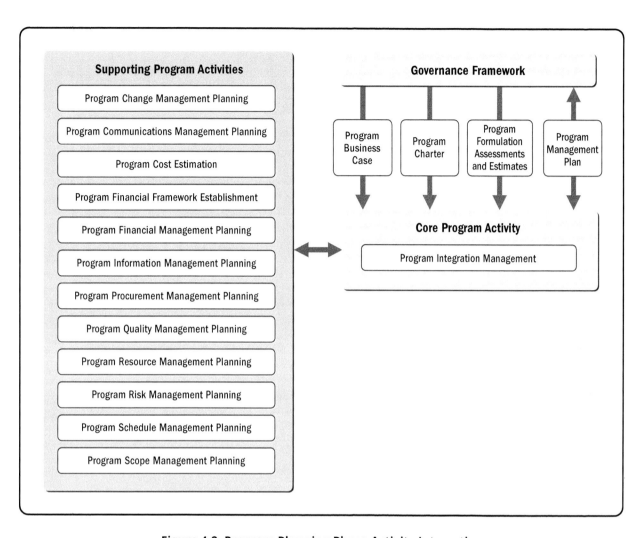

Figure 4-2. Program Planning Phase Activity Interaction

4.3 PROGRAM DELIVERY PHASE ACTIVITIES

Program delivery phase activities include program activities required for coordinating and managing the actual delivery of programs. These activities include change control, reporting, information distribution, cost, procurement, quality, and risk.

The program delivery phase provides supporting activities and processes that run throughout the program life cycle and are designed to provide the program management functions. Figure 4-3 illustrates how program delivery activities support program and component management.

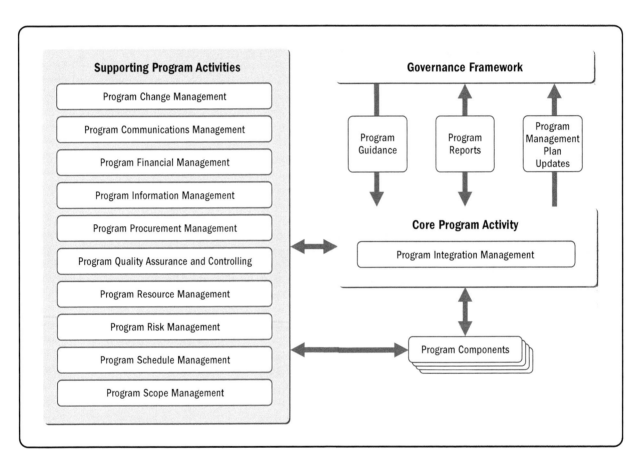

Figure 4-3. Program Delivery Phase Activity Interaction

4.3.1 PROGRAM DELIVERY MANAGEMENT

Program delivery management includes the management, oversight, integration, and optimization of the program components that should deliver the capabilities and benefits required for the organization to realize benefits and associated value. These activities are performed throughout the program delivery phase and relate to the initiation, change, transition, and closure of program components.

The role of the program manager should be to present a request to initiate a new component or project. This request is evaluated by the program steering committee, other group, or designated individual against the organization's approved selection criteria. A decision is made, utilizing the governance function, on whether the component should be initiated. If the component is approved, the program manager may need to redefine the priorities of existing program components to enable optimal resource allocation and management of interdependencies. Component initiation may be delayed or accelerated as defined by the program team and its needs. During the course of program delivery, change requests that fall within the program manager's authority level should be approved or rejected to manage performance and any changes to the program management plan.

As the program components reach the end of their respective life cycles or as planned program-level milestones are achieved, the program manager collaborates with the customer or sponsor to present a request to close or transition the component. This formal request is sent to the program steering committee, similar group, or designated individual for review and approval. The process of component transition includes making updates to the program roadmap. These updates reflect both go/no-go decisions and approved change requests that affect the high-level milestones, scope, or timing of major stages scheduled throughout the program.

4.3.2 PROGRAM PERFORMANCE MANAGEMENT

Program performance management activities are performed by both program- and project-level components during delivery management. These activities include designing a performance management framework that involves determining the optimum measurement, analysis, and dissemination of performance information to track progress against the program objectives and baselines to allow for data-driven governance and management. Continuous monitoring gives the program management team insight into the current health of the program and identifies areas that might require special attention. This monitoring and assessment determines if and when activities, such as corrective or preventive action, are needed to bring the program back into alignment with the strategic priorities.

It is necessary to manage changes at a strategic level and monitor changes in the progress of program components within the standardized project management practice that exists in the organization and the governance framework.

Program performance reports include a summary of the progress of all program components. They describe whether the program's goals can be met and benefits should be delivered according to plan. These reports provide current status information about what work has been accomplished; milestones and phase gates; what work remains to be completed; earned value; and risks, issues, and changes under consideration. Forecasts enable the program manager and other key stakeholders to assess the likelihood of achieving planned outcomes and to provide predictions of the program's future state based on the current information and knowledge available.

4.3.3 BENEFITS SUSTAINMENT AND PROGRAM TRANSITION

During this subphase, the stewardship of sustaining the benefits may need to transition to another organization, entity, or subsequent program to eventually operationalize the program's benefits. Benefits sustainment may be achieved through portfolio, program, or project outcomes. This activity transcends the scope of individual program components since this work is typically performed as the program is closed. During this subphase, the stewardship of sustaining the benefits may need to transition to another organization, entity, or subsequent program.

4.3.4 PROGRAM CHANGE MANAGEMENT

Program change management encompasses the activities whereby modifications to documents, deliverables, or baselines associated with the program are identified, documented, approved, or rejected. Program change management is a critical aspect of overall program delivery and should include monitoring factors internal and external to the program that might create the need for changes to the program.

A program change request is a formal proposal to modify any program document, deliverable, or baseline. Program change requests should be recorded in the program change log. The program change requests should be analyzed to determine their urgency and impact on program baseline elements and other program components. When there are multiple ways to implement the change, the costs, risks, interdependencies among program components, and other aspects of each option should be assessed in multidisciplinary aspects by all involved parties to enable selection of the approach most likely to deliver the program's intended benefits.

Once a decision on the program change request has been made by the program manager, program sponsor, program steering committee, or other designated authority as appropriate, and approval/rejection has been granted, program change control should carry out the request and make sure it is:

- ▶ Recorded in the program change log;
- ▶ Communicated to appropriate stakeholders, according to the program communications management plan; and
- ▶ Reflected in updates to component plans, including the financial management plan and the schedule management plan, as needed.

Change decisions should be in accordance with the defined escalation paths and program governance.

4.3.5 PROGRAM COMMUNICATIONS MANAGEMENT

Program communications management comprises the activities necessary for the timely and appropriate generation, collection, distribution, storage, retrieval, and ultimate disposition of program information. Program communications management includes coordination, direction, and support of component communications to provide alignment with the program's overall communications objectives. Program information is distributed to the receiving parties, including the clients, program sponsor, program steering committee, executives, component managers, and, in some cases, the public and press.

The outcomes of this activity include program communications regarding:

▶ Status information on the program, projects, subsidiary programs, or other work, including progress, cost information, risk analysis, and other information relevant to internal or external audiences;

▶ Notification of program change requests to the program and component teams, and the corresponding responses to the change requests;

▶ Program financial reports for internal or external stakeholders or for the purpose of public disclosure;

▶ External filings with government and regulatory bodies as prescribed by laws and regulations;

▶ Presentations before legislative bodies with the required prebriefs;

▶ Public announcements communicating public outreach information;

▶ Press releases;

▶ Social media articles and posts on internal and external company platforms such as LinkedIn or the company intranet and website; and

▶ Media interviews and benefits updates.

4.3.6 PROGRAM FINANCIAL MANAGEMENT

Once the program receives initial funding and begins paying expenses, the financial effort moves into tracking and managing the program's funds and expenditures. Monitoring the program's finances and controlling expenditures within budget are critical aspects of enabling the program to meet the goals of the funding agency or of the higher organization. A program where its costs exceed the planned budget may no longer satisfy the business case used to justify it, and may be subject to termination. Even minor overruns can be subject to audit and management oversight and should be justified. Typical financial management activities should be undertaken to identify factors that create changes to the baseline budget.

As part of this activity, payments are made in accordance with the contracts, with the financial infrastructure of the program, and with the status of the contract deliverables. Individual component budgets are closed when work is completed on each component. Throughout the program, as changes are approved that have significant cost impacts, the program's budget baseline is updated accordingly and the budget is rebaselined. New financial forecasts for the program are prepared on a regular basis and communicated in accordance with the program communications management plan. Similarly, approved changes, either to the program or to an individual component, are incorporated into the appropriate budget. All of these activities may result in updates to the program management plan.

4.3.7 PROGRAM INFORMATION MANAGEMENT

Program management involves the extensive exchange of information among the program management, component management, portfolio management, program stakeholders, and program steering committee functions of an organization. Managing this information, and making it available to support program communications, program management, or archiving, is a continuous task, especially in organizations pursuing numerous programs or programs that are complicated or complex.

Using the information management tools and processes established in the program information management plan, this activity collects, receives, organizes, and stores the documents and other information products created by program activities, program governance, and program components. Attention should be paid to the accuracy and timeliness of the information to avoid errors and incorrect decisions. The program information repository can be an invaluable aid to other program activities, particularly when there is a need to refer to past decisions or prepare analyses based on trends reflected in historical program information.

The outcomes of this activity might include updates to the program information repository and inputs to information distribution and program reporting.

4.3.7.1 Lessons Learned

Lessons learned are a compilation of the knowledge gained. This knowledge may be acquired from executing similar and relevant programs from the past or it may reside in public domain databases. Lessons learned are critical assets to be reviewed when updating the program stakeholder register, program benefits register, program risk register, program master schedule, and program communications management plan—or when considering major changes to the program management plan, including the introduction of new program components. The lessons learned register is updated when necessary, including at the completion of components and the end of the program. The inputs to the lessons learned register should be prioritized and key inputs should be discussed with the portfolio manager, program sponsor, and other key stakeholders.

4.3.8 PROGRAM PROCUREMENT MANAGEMENT

When program procurement is applicable, program managers utilize multiple tools and techniques to conduct program procurements, but the key objective of conducting program-level procurement is to set standards for the components. These standards may come in the form of qualified seller lists, prenegotiated contracts, blanket purchase agreements, and formalized proposal evaluation criteria.

One common structure used by the program manager is to direct all procurements to be centralized and conducted by a program-level team rather than assigning that responsibility to individual components.

Once the program standards are in place and the agreements and contracts are signed, administration and closeout may be transitioned to the components. The details of contract deliverables, requirements, deadlines, cost, and quality are handled at the component level, unless the contract impacts more than one component, such as equipment that is costly and will be used by more than one component in an agreement to share resources. The individual managers at the component level report the procurement results and closeouts to the program manager. Where contracts are administered at the program level, however, component managers coordinate or report deliverable acceptance, contract changes, and other contract issues with the program staff.

The program manager maintains visibility during procurement to enable the program budget to be expended properly to obtain program benefits.

4.3.9 PROGRAM QUALITY ASSURANCE AND CONTROL

Program quality assurance and control involves the activities related to the periodic evaluation of overall program quality to provide confidence that the program can comply with relevant quality policies and standards. Quality assurance involves not only program quality planning, but also meeting customer expectations and ensuring benefits can deliver value as defined and expected by the intended beneficiary. This quality review is the key deliverable of quality assurance—that the outcome of the program is satisfactorily rendered for the beneficiaries. Once the initial quality assurance specifications are decided upon in the program planning subphase, quality should be continuously monitored and analyzed. Programs often conduct quality assurance audits to make sure proper updates are performed. New government laws and regulations may create new quality standards. The program management team is responsible for implementing all required quality changes. The lengthy duration of programs often requires quality assurance updates throughout the program's life cycle. Program quality assurance focuses on cross-program, intercomponent quality relationships, and how one component's quality specification impacts another component's quality when they are interdependent. Program quality assurance also includes the analysis of the quality control results of the program components to see that overall program quality is delivered.

Program quality control involves the monitoring of specific components or program deliverables and results to determine if they meet the quality requirements and lead to benefits realization. The quality control activity contributes to the implementation of the quality plans at the project and subsidiary program levels, using quality reviews that should be performed with constituent component reviews. Quality control is performed throughout the duration of the program. Program results include product and service deliverables, management results and cost schedules, and performance, as well as the benefits realized by the end user. End-user satisfaction is a metric that should be obtained to gauge the program quality. The fitness for use of the benefits, products, or services delivered by the program is best evaluated by those who receive it. To that end, programs often use customer satisfaction surveys as one quality control measurement.

4.3.10 PROGRAM RESOURCE MANAGEMENT

Throughout program delivery, the program manager should oversee and adapt program resources to provide benefits delivery. Resource prioritization allows the program manager to prioritize the use of limited resources and to optimize their use across all components within the program. This prioritization often involves human resource planning to identify, document, and assign program roles and responsibilities to individuals or groups.

During program delivery, the need for staff, facilities, equipment, and other resources changes. The program manager manages resources at the program level and works with the component managers, who manage resources at the component level to balance the needs of the program with the availability of resources.

Resource prioritization decisions should be based on the guidelines in the program resource management plan. Since decisions to change existing program components or initiate new ones may have impacts on program resources, the program resource management plan may need to be adapted as a result.

Resources are often shared among different components within a program, and the program manager should work to ensure that the interdependencies do not cause delays in benefits delivery, which can be achieved by carefully controlling the schedule for scarce resources. The program manager enables resources to be released to other programs when they are no longer necessary for the current program.

The program manager may work with the component managers to see that the program's resource management plan accounts for changes in use of interdependent or scarce program resources.

The output of this activity includes updates to the program's resource management plan.

4.3.11 PROGRAM RISK MANAGEMENT

Throughout program delivery, the program manager needs to update the risk register and manage program risks (see Section 3.3.5.4.) to provide for benefits delivery. The program risk manager is responsible for ensuring implementation of risk management across all component projects, and reports to the program manager.

Risk monitoring is also conducted to determine whether:

▶ Program assumptions are still valid,

▶ Effective program risk management also requires coordination with component risk management functions,

▶ Effective crisis management is in place, and

▶ Unknown-unknowns, known-unknowns, and other ill-defined risks may materialize.

To respond to risks, the program manager identifies and directs actions to mitigate the negative consequences to enable realization of potential benefits and enhance opportunities. The program manager may hold management or contingency reserves at the program level to support risk responses. The program contingency reserve is not a substitute for the component contingency reserve, which is held at the component or portfolio level.

4.3.12 PROGRAM SCHEDULE MANAGEMENT

Program schedule management is the activity of enabling the program to produce the required capabilities and benefits on time. This activity includes tracking and monitoring the start and finish of all high-level component and program activities and milestones against the program master schedule's planned timelines. Updating the program master schedule and directing changes to individual component schedules are required to maintain an accurate and up-to-date program master schedule.

Program schedule management works closely with other program activities to identify variances to the schedules and direct corrective action when necessary. Program management is dependent on the alignment of program scope with cost and schedule, which are dependent on each other. Schedule control involves identifying not only slippages but also opportunities to accelerate program or component schedules and should be used for risk management. Program schedule risks should be tracked as part of the risk management activity.

The program master schedule should also be reviewed to assess the impact of component-level changes on other components and on the program itself. There may be a need to accelerate or decelerate components within the schedule to achieve program goals. Identification of both slippages and early deliveries are necessary as part of the overall program management function. Identification of early deliveries may provide opportunities for program acceleration. Approval of deviations to component schedules may be necessary to realize program benefits as a result of component performance deviations. Due to the complexity and potential long duration of programs, the program master schedule may need to be updated to include new components or remove components as a result of approved change requests to meet evolving program goals. The program management plan should be assessed for potential revision when there is significant change in the program master schedule.

The program schedule management activity includes updates to the program master schedule and program roadmap, and identification of schedule risks as outputs to the activity.

4.3.13 PROGRAM SCOPE MANAGEMENT

It is important for the program manager to manage scope as the program develops in order to achieve completion. Scope changes that have a significant impact on a component or the program may originate from stakeholders, components within the program, previously unidentified requirements issues, or external sources.

Program scope management should be exercised in line with the program change management and program scope management plans. This activity should capture requested scope changes, evaluate each requested change, determine the disposition of each requested change, communicate the decision to affected stakeholders, and record the change request and supporting details. Major change requests, when approved, may require updates to the program management plan and program scope statement.

The program manager is responsible for determining which components of the program are affected when a program scope change is requested, and should update the program work breakdown structure (WBS) accordingly. In very large programs, the number of components affected may be substantial and difficult to assess. Program managers should restrict their activities to managing scope only to the allocated level for components and avoid controlling component scope that has been further decomposed by the project manager or by subsidiary program managers.

4.4 PROGRAM CLOSURE PHASE ACTIVITIES

The program closure phase activities begin when the program components have delivered all their outputs and the program has begun to deliver its intended benefits. In some cases, the program steering committee might decide to bring a program to an early close before all components have been completed. In either case, the goal of the program activities during this phase is to release the program resources and support the transition of any remaining program outputs and assets, including its documents and databases, to ongoing organizational activities.

Figure 4-4 illustrates how program closure activities support program closure and transition to sustaining organizational operations.

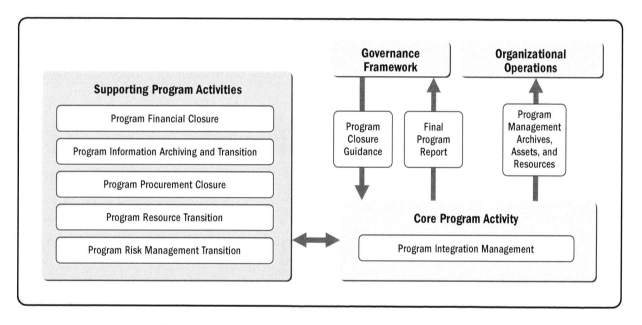

Figure 4-4. Program Closure Phase Activity Interaction

4.4.1 PROGRAM CLOSEOUT

A program is closed either because the program charter is fulfilled or internal/external conditions arise that bring the program to an early end. These conditions may include changes in the business case that no longer make the program necessary or a determination that the expected benefits cannot be achieved. During closeout, benefits may have been fully realized or they may continue to be realized and managed as part of organizational operations. Successful completion of the program is judged against the approved program business case, actual program outcomes, and the current goals and strategic objectives of the organization. All components should be completed or terminated, assigned resources released, and all contracts should be formally closed before the program is ended. Once these criteria have been met, the program should receive formal closure acceptance from the program steering committee or designated group or individual.

As part of the program governance plan, a final program report may be required to document critical information that can be applied to improve the potential for success of future programs and component projects. This final report may consist of:

▶ Formal closure acceptance,

▶ Benefits transition plan,

▶ Financial and performance assessments,

▶ Lessons learned,

▶ Successes and failures,

▶ Identified areas for improvement,

▶ Risk management outcomes,

▶ Risks that were unforeseen,

▶ Customer approval,

▶ Reason(s) for program closeout,

▶ Histories of all baselines, and

▶ Archive plan for the program documentation, program charter, program roadmap, and program management plan.

4.4.2 PROGRAM FINANCIAL CLOSURE

To enable program closeout, estimates may be required to determine the costs of sustaining benefits created by the program. It is important to verify that these costs are being captured. While many of these costs are captured in operations, maintenance, or other activities initiated in the program delivery phase as components are delivered, there may be residual activities required to oversee the ongoing benefits. This stewardship may be structured as an individual project or as a resulting program, or may be incorporated as new work under a separate portfolio or program or in new or existing operations. As the program nears completion, the program budget is closed and the final financial reports are communicated in accordance with the program communications management plan. Any unspent monies are returned to the funding organization.

Program financial transition is complete once sustainment budgets are developed, benefits are delivered, and sustainment has commenced.

4.4.3 PROGRAM INFORMATION ARCHIVING AND TRANSITION

For legal reasons, or to support ensuing operations or other programs, there may be a need to collect program records and organize them for archiving or for use by other elements of the organization. The scope of this activity may include collection and archiving of records as well as documentation from components.

Proper information management during program closure also includes the transfer of program knowledge to support the ongoing sustainment of program benefits by providing the new supporting organization with documentation, training, or materials. The program manager may assess the program's performance, collect observations from program team members, and provide a final lessons learned report that incorporates the individual findings from continuous lessons learned captured throughout the program/component activities. This report can inform the governance and management of other programs in the organization and help avoid pitfalls encountered during program delivery.

Lessons learned is a continuous process throughout the program journey and should be properly updated and documented with version systems until the program closure and final archive. The lessons learned is a vital source of information for the next program and helps in avoiding future issues, selecting better vendors, receiving better services, and improving estimation accuracy among the program team.

4.4.4 PROGRAM PROCUREMENT CLOSURE

Program procurement closure activities are those that formally close out each agreement of the program after making sure all deliverables have been satisfactorily completed, all payments have been made, and there are no outstanding contractual issues. In the case of a program that is closed early, program procurement closure manages the termination of active contracts to avoid unnecessary costs.

4.4.5 PROGRAM RESOURCE TRANSITION

It is important to enable program resources to be appropriately released as the program is being closed, which may involve the reallocation or reassignment of team members and funding to other initiatives or programs. Reassignment of resources at the component level may also include transitioning resources to another component already in execution or another program within the organization that requires a similar skill set. Refer to the *PMBOK® Guide* [1] for more information regarding resource disposition for component projects.

The efficient and appropriate release of program resources is an essential activity of program closure. At the program level, the program steering committee, other group, or designated individual releases resources as a part of activities leading to program closure approval.

The outputs of this activity include resources released to other organizational elements, the return or sale of purchased infrastructure, canceled leases and liabilities, and transfers of materials to reuse in other programs.

4.4.6 PROGRAM RISK MANAGEMENT TRANSITION

Although the program is closed, there may be remaining risks that could undermine the realization of benefits by the organization. Program risk management activities should transfer these risks, along with any supporting analysis and response information, to the appropriate organizational risk register. This may be managed by a different organizational group than the one intended to realize the benefits, such as an organizational program management office.

Appendix X1
Program Activities, Tools, and Techniques

This appendix provides examples of tasks and work conducted to support a program throughout the program life cycle. In addition to the information provided in this standard, further guidance on program management activities, tools, and techniques can be found in PMIstandards+®, a dynamic platform that is a companion to PMI content. Use the QR code below to find more related subject matter. PMI membership or a subscription is required.

X1.1 PROGRAM INFRASTRUCTURE DEVELOPMENT

Program infrastructure development is performed to investigate, assess, and plan the support structure that should assist the program in achieving its goals. This activity is initiated in the program definition phase and may be repeated again at any time during the program life cycle in order to update or modify the infrastructure.

The primary purpose of program infrastructure development is twofold. It establishes both the management and technical resources of the program and its components. This infrastructure refers to both personnel and program-specific tools, facilities, and finances used to manage the program.

Although the program manager is assigned during program definition, the program management core team is designated as part of establishing the program infrastructure. The core team members may not necessarily be assigned full-time to the program; these key stakeholders, however, are instrumental in determining and developing the program's infrastructure requirements.

For many programs, the program management office is a core part of the program infrastructure. It supports the management and coordination of the program and component work. The program management office also establishes consistent policies, standards, and training for programs in the organization. Another key element of the program infrastructure is the program management information system. A program management information system consists of tools used to collect, integrate, and communicate information critical to the management of one or more organizational programs. An effective program management information system incorporates the following:

- Software tools such as workspace chat, videoconferencing, file storage, and application integration;
- Documents, data, and knowledge repositories;
- Configuration management tools;
- Change management systems;
- Risk database and analysis tools;
- Financial management systems;
- Earned value management activities and tools;
- Requirements management activities and tools; and
- Other tools and activities as required.

The use of these resources should be separate and distinct from those required to manage the individual components within the program. The distinguishing factor is that most resources and program costs are managed at the component level instead of the program level.

X1.2 PROGRAM CHANGE ASSESSMENT

As part of program formulation, potential change management considerations are identified and assessed to help develop the program's business case. The program change assessment identifies sources of change, such as the volatility of the enterprise environmental factors (EEFs), the sensitivity of the proposed program's business case to changes in organizational strategy, and the possible frequency and magnitude of changes that may arise from components during program delivery. It then estimates the likelihood and possible impacts of the changes that may arise from these sources, and proposes measures that may be taken to enable the program to respond to such changes in a positive, rather than disruptive, way.

The output of this activity is the program change assessment, which is an input to the program business case, program charter, and program change management planning.

X1.3 PROGRAM COMMUNICATIONS ASSESSMENT

Program communications management is different from project communications management. Since it affects an array of stakeholders with varying communication needs, different communication approaches and methods of delivery are required.

An initial assessment of the program's communication needs is a key input to the program charter. Given the broad scope of a program, a wide range of stakeholders may be involved, and maintaining communications with internal and external stakeholders can prevent more serious problems from arising. It may be useful, as part of program formulation, to survey program stakeholders to identify their expectations for its outcome and their interests in staying informed and involved during its delivery.

The output of this activity is the program communications assessment, which is an input to the program business case, program charter, stakeholder engagement plan, and program communications management planning.

X1.4 PROGRAM INITIAL COST ESTIMATION

A critical element of the program's business case is an estimate of its overall cost and an assessment of the level of confidence in this estimate. An initial cost estimate is prepared in the program definition phase to determine the cost of its planning and delivery. This initial rough-order-of-magnitude estimate allows financial decision makers to decide if the program should be funded. Because of the limited information, time, and resources available, it may be difficult to develop a highly detailed or accurate cost estimate. Often the numbers will only be accurate to a rough order of magnitude. Given these challenges, it may also be useful to identify the nature and sources of those costs that cannot be estimated.

The outcome of this activity is the program's initial cost estimate, which is an input to the program business case, program charter, and detailed program cost estimation during program planning.

X1.5 PROGRAM INFORMATION MANAGEMENT ASSESSMENT

A program can generate a large amount of documentation, data, and other records throughout its life cycle. How easily this information can be collected, shared, and maintained may have a significant effect on both program team efficiency and how the program is perceived by its stakeholders. The information management needs of the program should be considered as part of program formulation, so that possible financial, organizational, maturity of project management culture, or resource implications can be assessed.

The output of this activity is the program information management assessment, which is an input to the program business case, program charter, and program information management planning during program planning.

X1.6 PROGRAM PROCUREMENT ASSESSMENT

An assessment of the procurement needs of a program can be a valuable input to the program charter. Although procurement policies and practices are typically part of the organizational or environmental factors that exist before the program is authorized, there are cases (e.g., programs involving public–private partnership or programs involving organizations or work in multiple countries) where the program itself presents unique procurement challenges. A program procurement assessment should be prepared during program definition, when procurement presents special challenges or represents a significant level of effort during program delivery.

The output of this activity is the program procurement management assessment, which is an input to the program business case, program charter, and program procurement management planning during program planning.

X1.7 PROGRAM QUALITY ASSESSMENT

An assessment of quality constraints, expectations, risks, and controls should be included as part of program formulation. Organizational or regulatory quality standards may act as important constraints on program delivery, particularly in the case of a compliance program. Expectations about the quality of program outputs may serve as important inputs to determine program costs and required program infrastructure and resources. The ability of program suppliers to comply with quality standards may also be an important consideration for the program procurement and risk assessments. Finally, the need for program quality reviews or audits may be considered important to enable program governance.

The output of this activity is the program quality assessment, which is an input to the program business case, program charter, and program quality management planning during program planning.

X1.8 PROGRAM RESOURCE REQUIREMENTS ESTIMATION

The resources required to plan and deliver a program include people, office space, laboratories, data centers or other facilities, equipment of all types, software, online collaboration tools, platforms, and office supplies. An estimate of the required resources—particularly staff and facilities, which may have long lead times or affect ongoing activities—is required to prepare the program business case and should be reflected in the program charter.

The outcome of this activity is the program resource requirements estimate, which is an input to the program business case, program charter, and program resource management planning during program planning.

X1.9 PROGRAM INITIAL RISK ASSESSMENT

A program risk is an uncertain event or series of events or conditions that, if they occur, may affect the success of the program. Positive risks are often referred to as opportunities and negative risks as threats. These risks arise from the program components and their interactions with one another, such as a change in strategy; presence and enhancement of program complexity that affects governance; stakeholder engagement; delivery of program benefits; the rise of technical, structural, temporal, or managerial complexity; schedule; or cost constraints.

Two aspects of risk should be assessed during program definition. First, an identification of the key risks that the program may encounter, and their relative likelihood and impact, should be developed as an input to the program business case and the program charter. Second, an assessment of the organization's willingness to accept and deal with risks—sometimes referred to as its risk appetite—is essential to understanding the level of effort that may be required to monitor and assess risks during program delivery.

The output of this activity is the program initial risk assessment, which is an input to the program business case, program initial cost estimate, program charter, program roadmap, and program risk management planning during program planning.

X1.10 PROGRAM SCHEDULE ASSESSMENT

An assessment of expectations for delivery dates and benefits milestones should be part of the program charter. This initial assessment should also state the level of confidence in the assessment of activity durations and identify where alternative activities could be initiated if activities run into excessive delays.

The outcome of this activity is the program schedule assessment, which is an input to the program business case, program charter, program management plan, and program schedule management planning.

X1.11 PROGRAM SCOPE ASSESSMENT

Program scope defines the work required to deliver a benefit (major product, service, or result with specified features and functions), along with major management activities at the program level. Program scope management comprises the activities that define, develop, oversee, and verify program scope. Scope management aligns the program scope with the program's goals and objectives. It includes work decomposition into deliverable component products designed to deliver the associated benefits.

An assessment of program scope, which includes boundaries, links to other programs/projects, and ongoing activities, is required as part of the program charter and to support initial cost, change, resource, risk, and schedule assessments.

This initial program scope assessment develops the program scope statement from the program goals and objectives. This input to the program charter can be obtained from the program sponsor or stakeholders through the portfolio management or stakeholder alignment activities.

The outcome of this activity is the program scope assessment, which is an input to the program charter.

X1.12 PROGRAM CHANGE MANAGEMENT PLANNING

A change management activity should be established to administer changes during the course of the program. The program change management plan is a component of the program management plan that establishes program change management principles and procedures, including the approach for capturing requested changes, evaluating each requested change, determining the disposition of each requested change, communicating a decision to impacted stakeholders, documenting the change request and supporting details, and authorizing funding and work. It is important to mention that the plan should focus on how to evaluate the impact of a change (e.g., change in an organization, including program sponsor and program steering committee; change in a cost; change in a component; change in the program management plan; change in a technology; etc.) on the program outcomes and, therefore, on the benefits expected by the stakeholders. Based on that assumption, the program steering committee should agree on the level of program change thresholds that should trigger the change process.

The outcomes of this activity include the program change management plan and program change thresholds.

X1.13 PROGRAM COMMUNICATIONS MANAGEMENT PLANNING

The importance of managing communications internal and external to the program should not be underestimated or overlooked. Program managers spend a significant amount of time and effort communicating with the program stakeholders, including the program team, component teams, component managers, customers, program steering committee, executives, and program sponsor. Significant problems may occur if sufficient effort is not committed to communications. Program communications management includes activities for the timely and appropriate generation, collection, distribution, storage, retrieval, and ultimate disposition of program information. These activities provide the critical links between people and information that are necessary for communications and decision-making.

Program communications management planning is the activity of determining the information and communication needs of the program stakeholders, based on who needs what information, when they need it, how it will be given to them, and by whom. The program communications management plan is the component of the program management plan that describes how, when, and by whom information will be administered and disseminated. Communication requirements should be clearly defined to facilitate the transfer of information between the program and its components and from the program to the appropriate stakeholders with the appropriate content and delivery methods. Communication requirements specific to particular stakeholders should be included in the stakeholder register.

As the program progresses, other components are added and new stakeholders become known and addressed. This distinction should be considered when planning communications. Cultural and language differences, time zones, and other factors associated with globalization should be considered when developing the program communications management plan. Although complex, program communications management planning is vital to the success of any program.

The outcomes of this activity include the program communications management plan and communication requirements inputs to the stakeholder register.

X1.14 PROGRAM COST ESTIMATION

Program cost estimation is performed throughout the course of the program and is a fundamental part of the overall business case justification. Many organizations use a tiered funding process with a series of go/no-go decisions at each major stage of the program. They agree to an overall financial management plan and commit to a budget only for the next stage at each governance milestone.

A weight or probability may be applied, based on the quantitative risk analysis and complexity of the work to be performed, in order to derive a confidence factor in the estimate. Statistical techniques, such as Monte Carlo simulation, may also be used. This confidence factor is used to determine the potential range of program costs. When determining program costs, decision makers should consider not only the development and implementation costs but also sustainment costs that may occur after the program is completed. Calculating the full life cycle costs, including transition and sustainment costs, results in the total cost of ownership. Total cost of ownership is considered to be relative to the expected benefit of one program against another to derive a funding decision. There are numerous estimating techniques to derive program cost estimates.

Program cost estimates should also identify any constraints and assumptions upon which the estimates are made, as these constraints and/or assumptions may prove unfounded in the course of program delivery and require reconsideration of the program business case or revision of the program management plan.

Finally, program cost estimation can support or guide cost estimation at the component level. Any prevailing program-level cost estimation guidance intended for use at the component level should be documented and communicated to component managers.

The outcomes of this activity include program cost estimates, program cost estimation assumptions, and component cost estimation guidelines.

X1.15 PROGRAM FINANCIAL FRAMEWORK ESTABLISHMENT

The type of program and the funding structure dictate the financial environment for the duration of the program. Funding models vary, including those that are:

▶ Funded entirely within a single organization,

▶ Managed within a single organization but funded separately,

▶ Funded and managed entirely from outside the parent organization, and

▶ Supported with internal and external sources of funding.

Often the program itself may be funded by one or more sources, and the program components may be funded by altogether different sources. In addition to funding sources, the timing of funding has a direct impact on a program's ability to perform. To a much greater extent than for projects, program costs occur earlier (often years earlier) than their related benefits. The objective of financing in program development is to obtain funds to bridge the gap between paying out monies for development and obtaining the benefits of the programs. Covering this large, negative cash balance is a key challenge in program financing. Due to the large amount of money involved in most programs, the funding organization is rarely a passive partner but instead has significant inputs to program management and decisions made by the business leads, technical leads, and the program manager. Due to this, communications with the program sponsor and other key stakeholders should be proactive, as complete as possible, and timely.

A program financial framework is a high-level, initial plan for coordinating available funding, determining constraints, and determining how funding is allocated. The financial framework defines and describes the program funding flows so the money is spent as required to realize the program benefits and achieve transition.

As the program financial framework is developed and analyzed, changes may be identified that impact the original business case justifying the program. Based on these changes, the business case should be revised with full involvement of the decision makers (see Section 3.3.1).

It is important to understand the specific and unique needs of the program sponsor and the funding organizations' representatives with regard to financial arrangements. The program communications management and stakeholder engagement plans may need updates to reflect these needs.

Financial framework establishment usually occurs during the program formulation subphase as part of program definition.

The outputs of this activity include the program financial framework, business case updates, and updates to the program communications management and stakeholder engagement plans.

X1.16 PROGRAM FINANCIAL MANAGEMENT PLANNING

Program financial management comprises the activities related to identifying the program's financial sources and resources, integrating the budgets of the program components, developing the overall budget for the program, and controlling costs during the program. In this context, the program financial management plan is a component of the program management plan that documents the program's financial aspects: funding schedules and milestones, initial budget, contract payments and schedules, financial reporting activities and mechanisms, and the financial metrics.

The program financial management plan expands upon the program financial framework and describes the management of items such as risk reserves, potential cash flow problems, international exchange rate fluctuations, future interest rate increases or decreases, inflation, currency devaluation, local laws regarding finances, trends in material costs, and contract incentive and penalty clauses. The plan should include an approval or authorization process to allocate funds for program components. For programs that are funded internally, either through retained earnings, bank loans, or the sale of bonds, the program manager should consider scheduled contract payments, inflation, the aforementioned factors, and other environmental factors. When developing the program financial management plan, the program manager should also include any component payment schedules, operational costs, and infrastructure costs.

Developing the program's initial budget involves compiling all available financial information and listing income and payment schedules in sufficient detail, so the program's costs can be tracked as part of the program budget. Once baselined, the budget becomes the primary financial target that the program is measured against.

It is important to develop financial metrics by which the program's benefits are measured. Developing these metrics is usually a challenge as cause-and-effect relationships are often difficult to establish in an endeavor the size and length of a program. One of the tasks of the program team and the program steering committee is to establish and validate these financial performance indicators.

As changes to cost, schedule, and scope occur throughout the duration of the program, these metrics are measured against the initial metrics used to approve the program. Decisions to continue, cancel, or modify the program are based, in part, on the results of these financial measures. Program financial risks that are identified as part of the financial management plan should be incorporated into the program risk register.

The outcomes of this activity include:

▶ Program financial management plan,

▶ Initial program budget,

▶ Program funding schedules,

▶ Component payment schedules,

▶ Program operational costs,

▶ Inputs to the program risk register, and

▶ Program financial metrics.

X1.17 PROGRAM PROCUREMENT MANAGEMENT PLANNING

Program procurement management is the application of the knowledge, skills, tools, and techniques necessary to acquire products and services to meet the needs of the overall program and the constituent projects and components. Program procurement management planning addresses the activities necessary to acquire products and services, and therefore, the specific procurement needs that are unique to managing the overall program and the needs of the constituent components. The program procurement management plan is a component of the program management plan that describes how the program can acquire goods and services from outside of the performing organization.

A program manager should understand the resources required for the delivery of benefits expected of the program. Techniques, such as make-or-buy decisions and program WBS charts, aid in this activity. The program manager needs to be cognizant of the available funding and needs of all components.

Early and intensive planning is critical for program procurement management. Throughout the planning activity, the program manager looks across all program components and develops a comprehensive plan that optimizes the procurements to meet program objectives and for the delivery of program benefits. To do this, program procurement management addresses commonalities and differences for the various procurements across the program scope and determines:

▶ Whether some of the common needs of several individual components could best be met with one overall procurement rather than several separate procurement actions;

▶ The best mix of the types of procurement contracts planned across the program (at the component level, a particular type of contract [e.g., firm fixed price] may appear to be the best procurement solution, but a different contract type [e.g., incentive fee] may be optimal for that same procurement when viewed at the program level);

▶ The best program-wide approach to competition (e.g., the risks of sole source contracts in one area of the program can be balanced with the different risks associated with full and open competition in other areas of the program); and

▶ The best program-wide approach to balancing specific external regulatory mandates. For example, rather than setting aside a certain percentage of each contract in the program to meet a small business mandate, it may be optimal to award one complete contract to achieve the same mandate.

This analysis may include requests for information (RFIs), feasibility studies, trade studies, and market analyses to determine the best fit of solutions and services to meet the specific needs of the program.

Due to the inherent need to optimize program procurement management and the requirements to adhere to all legal and financial obligations, it is essential that all personnel responsible for procurement at the component level work closely together, especially during the planning phase.

The outcomes of this activity include program procurement standards, the program procurement management plan, and program budget and financial plan updates.

X1.18 PROGRAM QUALITY MANAGEMENT PLANNING

Program quality management planning identifies the organizational or regulatory quality standards that are relevant to the program as a whole, and specifies how to satisfy them across the program. The program quality management plan is a component of the program management plan that describes how an organization's quality policies should be implemented. Often within a program, there are many differing quality assurance requirements as well as differing test and quality control methods and activities. Program quality management consists of the activities of the performing organization that determine program quality policies, objectives, and responsibilities. Program quality management aims to align these varying requirements and control methods, and may add additional ones to enable overall program quality. It is good practice for the program manager to document the overall program's quality objectives and principles in a quality policy that is shared with all program components.

Program management is responsible for the planning of the proper quality assurance criteria throughout the life cycle of the program, which may exceed the timelines of the individual components. New quality control tools, activities, and techniques may be introduced into the program and employed when appropriate. An example of this is when new laws are enacted or new components are introduced during the program's life cycle.

When initiating the program, the cost of the level of quality requirements should be evaluated and incorporated into the business plan. Quality is a variable cost in all components and should be considered as such in the program quality management plan. It is beneficial to analyze program quality in order to evaluate it across the program with the goal of combining quality tests and inspections to reduce costs, where feasible. If the tests are not coordinated, products and deliverables could be tested several times throughout a program and a cost incurred for no valid reason. It should be noted that the output of this activity is a quality management plan, which provides the quality assurance measures and quality controls that are incorporated into the program and the methods of inspection based on the program scope.

Quality management should be considered when defining all program activities as well as for every deliverable and service. For example, when developing a program resource management plan, it is recommended that a program quality manager participate in the planning activity to verify that quality activities and controls are applied and flow down to all the components, including those performed by subcontractors.

The outcome of this activity is a program quality management plan that may contain:

▶ Program quality policy;

▶ Program quality standards;

▶ Program quality estimates of costs;

▶ Quality metrics, service-level agreements, or memorandums of understanding;

▶ Quality checklists; and

▶ Quality assurance and control specifications.

X1.19 PROGRAM RESOURCE MANAGEMENT PLANNING

Resource management at the program level is different from resource management at the component level; a program manager should work within the bounds of uncertainty and balance the needs of the components for which they are responsible. Program resource management enables required resources (people, equipment, materials, etc.) to be made available to the component managers to enable the delivery of benefits for the program.

Resource management planning involves identifying existing resources and the need for additional resources. In the case of human resources, the sum of resources needed to successfully complete each component can be less than the total quantity of resources needed to complete the program, because the resources can be reallocated among components as the components are completed. The program manager analyzes the availability of each resource in terms of both capacity and capability, and determines how these resources should be allocated across components to avoid overcommitment or inadequate support. Historical information may be used to determine the types of resources that were required for similar projects and programs.

The resource management plan is a component of the program management plan that forecasts the expected level of resource use across the program components, and relative to the program master schedule, to allow the program manager to identify potential resource shortfalls or conflicts over the use of scarce or constrained resources. The plan also describes the guidelines for making program resource prioritization decisions and resolving resource conflicts.

When resources are unavailable within the program, the program manager calls upon the larger organization for assistance. When necessary, the program manager should work with the organization to develop a statement of work (SOW) to contract the necessary resources.

The outcomes of this activity include program resource requirements and the program resource management plan.

X1.20 PROGRAM RISK MANAGEMENT PLANNING

Program risk management planning identifies how to approach and conduct risk management activities for a program by considering its components. The principles for risk management should be applied as outlined in *The Standard for Risk Management in Portfolios, Programs, and Projects* [6]. The risk management plan is a component of the program management plan that describes how risk management activities should be structured and performed.

Planning risk management activities provides that the level, type, and visibility of risk management are appropriate, based on the risks and importance of the program to the organization. It identifies the resources and time required for risk management activities. In addition, it establishes an agreed-upon basis for evaluating risks.

The program risk management planning activity should be conducted early in the program definition phase. It is crucial for the successful performance of other activities described in this section. It may also need to be repeated whenever major changes occur in the program. A key outcome of this activity is the program risk register, which is the document in which risks are recorded together with the results of risk analysis and risk response planning. The program risk register is a living document that is updated as program risks and risk responses change during program delivery.

It is essential to define risk profiles of organizations to construct the most suitable approach to managing program risks, adjusting risk sensitivity, and monitoring risk criticality. Risk targets and risk thresholds influence the program management plan. Risk profiles may be expressed in policy statements or revealed in actions. These actions may highlight organizational willingness to embrace high-threat situations or a reluctance to forgo high-opportunity choices. Market factors that apply to the program and its components should be included as environmental factors. The culture of the organization and its stakeholders also plays a role in shaping the approach to risk management.

Organizations may have predefined approaches to risk management such as risk categories, risk breakdown structures, common definitions of concepts and terms, risk statement formats, standard templates, roles and responsibilities, and authority levels for decision-making. Lessons learned from executing similar programs in the past are also critical assets to be reviewed as a component of establishing an effective risk management plan.

The outcomes from this activity include the program risk management plan and the program risk register.

X1.21 PROGRAM SCHEDULE MANAGEMENT PLANNING

The program schedule management planning activity determines the order and timing of the components needed to produce the program benefits, estimates the amount of time required to accomplish each one, identifies significant milestones during the performance of the program, and documents the outcomes of each milestone. A program schedule should be developed collaboratively with components as component schedules are elaborated. Program components include projects, subsidiary programs, and other work undertaken to deliver the program's scope.

Program schedule management planning begins with the program scope management plan and the program work breakdown structure (WBS), which define how the program components are expected to deliver the program's outputs and benefits. The initial program master schedule is often created before the detailed schedules of the individual components are available. The program's delivery date and major milestones are developed using the program management plan and the program charter.

The program master schedule is the top-level program planning document that defines the individual component schedules and dependencies among the program components (individual components and program-level activities) required to achieve the program goals. It should include those component milestones that represent an output to the program or share interdependency with other components.

The program master schedule should also include activities that are unique to the program including, but not limited to, activities related to stakeholder engagement (see Section 3.5), program-level risk mitigation, and program-level reviews. The program master schedule determines the timing of individual components, enables the program manager to determine when benefits should be delivered by the program, and identifies external dependencies of the program. The first draft of a program master schedule often only identifies the order and start and end dates of components and their key interdependencies with other components. Later, it may be enriched with more intermediate component results as the component schedules are developed.

Once the high-level program master schedule is determined, the dates for each individual component are identified and used to develop the component's schedule. These dates often act as a constraint at the component level. When a component has multiple deliverables upon which other components rely, those deliverables and interdependencies should be reflected in the overall program master schedule. When a program is established over a set of existing components, the program master schedule needs to incorporate the milestones and deliverables from the individual component schedules.

The schedule model principles outlined in the *Practice Standard for Scheduling* [16] should also be applied to the program master schedule. Maintaining a logic-based program network diagram and monitoring the critical path for component outputs with interdependencies is essential to the management of the program master schedule, while focusing on benefits realization (see Section 3.4) based on deliverables along the critical path.

The program schedule management plan is a component of the program management plan that establishes the criteria and activities for developing and overseeing the schedule. The program schedule management plan should include guidance on how changes to schedule baselines are to be coordinated and controlled across program components. The program master schedule identifies the agreed-upon sequence of component deliverables to facilitate planning of the individual component deliveries and expected benefits. It provides the program team/stakeholders with a visual representation of how the program is going to be delivered throughout its life cycle (see Section 3.8). The program master schedule is a living document and provides the program manager with a mechanism to identify risks and escalate component issues that may affect the program goals.

Program schedule risk inputs that are identified as part of the program master schedule development should be incorporated into the program risk register. These risks may be a result of component dependencies within the schedule or external factors identified as a result of the agreed-upon program schedule management plan. The program schedule management plan may establish scheduling standards that apply to all program components.

The program roadmap should periodically be assessed and updated to provide alignment between the program roadmap and program master schedule. Changes in the program master schedule may require changes in the program management plan, which should be reflected in the program master schedule.

The outcomes of this activity include the program schedule management plan, program master schedule, inputs to the program risk register, and updates to the program management plan.

X1.22 PROGRAM SCOPE MANAGEMENT PLANNING

Program scope management planning includes all of the activities involved in planning and aligning the program scope with the program's goals and objectives. It includes work decomposition into deliverable component products designed to deliver the associated benefits. The objective is to develop a detailed program scope statement, break down the program work into deliverable components, and develop a plan for managing the scope throughout the program.

Program scope is typically described in the form of expected benefits or outcomes to the sponsor organization and target publics, but may also be described as user stories or scenarios, depending on the type of program. Program scope encompasses all benefits to be delivered by the program, which are reflected in the form of a program work breakdown structure (WBS).

A program WBS is a deliverable-oriented hierarchical decomposition encompassing the total scope of the program and includes the deliverables to be produced by the constituent components. Elements not in the program WBS are outside the scope of the program. The program WBS includes, but is not limited to, program management artifacts such as plans, procedures, standards, processes, program management deliverables, and program management office support deliverables. The program WBS provides an overview of the program and shows how each component contributes to the objectives of the program. Decomposition stops at the level of control required by the program manager (typically to the first one or two levels of a component). The program WBS serves as the framework for developing the program master schedule and defines the program manager's management control points. It is an essential tool for building realistic schedules, developing cost estimates, and organizing work. It also provides the framework for reporting, tracking, and controlling.

Program-level deliverables should be clearly linked to benefits and focus on those activities associated with stakeholder engagement, program-level management—as opposed to management within its components—and component oversight and integration. Program scope includes scope that is decomposed and allocated into components. Care should be taken to avoid decomposing component-level scope into details that overlap the component managers' responsibilities.

Once the scope is developed, a plan for managing, documenting, and communicating scope changes should be developed during the program definition phase. The program scope management plan is a component of the program management plan that describes how the scope will be defined, developed, monitored, controlled, and verified.

The outcomes of this activity include the program scope statement, program scope management plan, and the program WBS.

X1.23 PROGRAM REPORTING

Program reporting is a critical element of program communications, as it supports both the governance framework and stakeholder engagement. Program reporting is the activity of consolidating performance- and reporting-related data to provide stakeholders with information about how resources are being used to deliver program benefits. Program reporting aggregates all information across projects, subsidiary programs, and program activities to provide a clear picture of the program as a whole.

This information is conveyed to the stakeholders by means of the information distribution activity to provide the needed status and deliverable information. Additionally, this information is communicated to program team members and its constituent components to provide general and background information about the program. Communication should be a two-way information flow. Any communications from customers or stakeholders regarding the program should be gathered by program management, analyzed, and distributed back within the program as required.

The outcomes of this activity might include reports required by program sponsors or program agreements, including formats and reporting frequency; customer feedback requests; and periodic reports and presentations, including dashboards required by C-level executives.

X1.24 PROGRAM COST BUDGETING

Since programs are, by definition, composed of multiple components, program budgets should include the costs for each individual component as well as costs for the resources to manage the program itself. The baselined program budget is the primary financial target that the program is measured against. The majority of the program's cost is attributable to the individual components within the program and not to managing the program itself. When contractors are involved, the details of the budget come from the contracts. The cost of program management and supporting program activities is added to the initial budget figure before a baseline budget can be prepared.

Two important parts of the budget are:

▶ Program payment schedules, and

▶ Component payment schedules.

The program payment schedules identify the schedules and milestones where funding is received by the funding organization. The component payment schedules indicate how and when contractors are paid, in accordance with the contract provisions. Once the baseline is determined, the program management plan is updated.

The outcomes of this activity might include updates to the program budget baseline, program payment schedules, and component payment schedules.

X1.25 COMPONENT COST ESTIMATION

Because programs have a significant element of uncertainty, not all program components may be known when the initial order-of-magnitude estimates are calculated during the program definition phase. In addition, given the typically long duration of a program, the initial estimates may need to be updated to reflect the current environment and cost considerations. It is good practice to calculate an estimate as close to the beginning of a work effort as possible. This way, if the cost of the output is lower than originally planned, the program manager may present an opportunity to the program sponsor for additional products that may need to be acquired later in the program. Conversely, if the cost is significantly higher, a change request may be generated. In the approval activity, the benefit of additional products can be weighed against the new cost to determine the proper action.

Cost estimates for the individual components within the program are developed. The component costs are baselined and become the budget for that particular component. When a contractor is performing this component, this cost is written into the contract.

The outcomes of this activity include component cost estimates.

Appendix X2
Fifth Edition Changes

X2.1 ABOUT THIS APPENDIX

To fully understand the changes that have been made to the structure and content of *The Standard for Program Management*—Fifth Edition, it is important to be aware of the update committee's objectives as well as the evolution of the standard.

Through the process of updating the fourth edition of this standard, it became clear that the importance of program management as an organizational competency has generated the need to maintain the lines of distinction between *The Standard for Program Management* and other core PMI standards, including *A Guide to the Project Management Body of Knowledge* (*PMBOK® Guide*) [1] and *The Standard for Portfolio Management* [3]. It was also an opportunity to build on the shift from process-based standards to principle-based standards by elaborating and identifying key principles of the program management discipline. The fifth edition development team continued down a similar path expressed in earlier editions and focused primarily on fine-tuning the principles and concepts that make up the standard, as well as ensuring consistency and alignment with updates to other foundational standards and applicable practice guides.

With this in mind, the content has been further rearranged to allow a streamlined approach to reading and use of the standard. Specific updates were made to reflect current trends in program management throughout the standard.

X2.2 OBJECTIVES

Specifically, the update committee's objectives included:

▶ Transition the product more fully from a process-based document to a principle-based document,

▶ Address and incorporate adaptive approaches into the product, and

▶ Introduce greater flexibility in its framework so that it may be implemented and tailored for a wider array of business needs and environments.

X2.3 APPROACH

To prepare the current update, the project committee developed an approach to the revision that incorporated a number of important strategies and principles, including format and layout (Section X2.3.1) and program management content (Section X2.3.2).

X2.3.1 FORMAT AND LAYOUT

When first encountering *The Standard for Program Management*—Fifth Edition, readers will immediately notice fundamental modifications to the format and layout of the standard. There were a number of crucial factors considered during the design of the framework for the fifth edition that will be beneficial as background information for readers familiar with earlier editions and will help explain the transition from the format of the fourth edition. To explain the current framework, a summary of the evolution of the standard from the first edition to the present is provided:

▶ **First edition.** When it was published, the first edition of *The Standard for Program Management* presented three key themes that captured the prevailing understanding of program management work. These themes included stakeholder management, program governance, and benefits management. Accompanying the themes was the definition of the program management life cycle. This life cycle was integrated into the initial chapters of the standard and further elaborated in the later chapters. This framework presents a decidedly "domain-oriented" approach to the standard; to the definition of program management work; and to the role of the program manager.

▶ **Second edition.** The second edition of *The Standard for Program Management* retained some discussion of the three program management themes described in the first edition. Many of the updates, however, focused on expanding the presence of the program management life cycle. This approach positioned the program management life cycle as the predominant thread throughout the entire standard document. In addition, a structure for the standard was adopted that mirrored the layout and format of the PMI project management standard, the *PMBOK® Guide* [1]. Within this structure, the program standard described specific program management Process Groups and Knowledge Areas. With this framework in place, the second edition revealed a clear, life-cycle-based "process orientation" to the presentation of program management work and the role of the program manager.

▶ **Third edition.** Considering the previous two editions, emphasis for the third edition was on usefulness and readability. Careful analysis of the most effective elements of the earlier editions resulted in a decision to change from the second edition's structure that paralleled the *PMBOK® Guide*'s [1] Process Groups, Knowledge Areas, and inputs/tools and techniques/outputs in favor of the domain-oriented presentation of the first edition.

Within the third edition, the following key changes were made:

▷ Return to the domain orientation of the first edition,

▷ Focus on the program management performance domains presented in the role delineation study,

▷ Benefits of the learnings and advancements derived from both previous editions of *The Standard for Program Management,* and

▷ Alignment to, and recognition of, other standards and writings in program management from outside the United States.

- **Fourth edition.** It was determined that significant changes between the third and fourth editions were not necessary, and changes instead focused on addressing deferred comments from the third edition update as well as comments submitted by subject matter experts through an internal review and exposure draft process. The major changes in the fourth edition included:

  ▷ Provision of updated definitions of program and program management;

  ▷ Expansion of various sections to address important topics of key program roles, program complexity and interdependency, program risk strategy, program stakeholder mapping, and program stakeholder communication;

  ▷ Alignment with recent PMI publications for consistency in description of roles in program governance;

  ▷ Introduction of life cycle phases with clarity in the nomenclature used to describe each phase; and

  ▷ Harmonization and alignment across the sections in the standard, and removal of duplicate or redundant artifacts.

- **Fifth edition.** This edition presents new content that builds and expands upon previous concepts presented in the earlier editions. The content has been further rearranged to allow a streamlined approach to reading and use of the standard. Specific updates were done to reflect current trends in program management throughout the standard and support use of the dynamic PMIstandards+® content platform. Specifically, the changes are summarized in Table X2-1.

Table X2-1. Fifth Edition High-Level Changes

Change Applied	Description
Updated Section 1 to include all introductory elements.	Absorbed key introductory elements from Section 2 that were applicable to the program management discipline and not just program management domains. Expanded the introduction to include specific details of new identified principles. Comparisons of program management with project management and/or portfolio management have been removed as dynamic content to be placed in PMIstandards+®.
Reorganized and renumbered sections for streamlined presentation of the standard.	Standard format updated with content presented in four main sections that cover the following: • **Section 1: Program Management Introduction.** Introduces all aspects of the program management discipline and concepts that are applicable to all types of programs, including general information on program roles and descriptions. • **Section 2: Program Management Principles.** New section that identifies and elaborates key program management principles for consideration by program management practitioners. • **Section 3: Program Management Performance Domains.** This section collects all the information found in the standard relevant to program management performance domains. This is presented in one section for ease of reference and distinction of principles, domains, and activities. • **Section 4: Program Activities.** This section contains all information on core and supporting program activities.
Introduction of new Section 2 for program management principles.	Added new section to support full transition from a process-based to a principle-based standard. Elaborated and identified key principles of program management. Program management principles: • Stakeholders • Change • Benefits Realization • Leadership • Synergy • Risk • Team of Teams • Governance
Section 2, Section 3, Section 4, Section 5, Section 6, and Section 7 all refined and merged into Section 3.	All content for performance domains has been brought under one section and further streamlined to remove requirements that may not be applicable to all programs or development approaches.
New content added.	New Collaboration performance domain has been introduced and incorporated throughout the standard. Relationship of the new domain to other domains is captured in the introduction.
Revised Section 7 as part of its merger into a revised Section 3 and Section 4.	The Life Cycle Management performance domain has been rearranged to focus on the program life cycle phases. Content for integration management has been classified as a core program activity and was moved to a revised Section 4 on program activities.
Revised Section 8 as part of the creation of a new Section 4 and Appendix X1.	The section on program activities has been rearranged to incorporate integration management as a supporting program activity. Supporting activity examples or specific methods that are variable across different types of programs have been moved to an appendix for further information on tools and techniques in program activities.
New Appendix X1 created.	New appendix created containing subcontent from Sections 7 and 8 that was specific to types of programs or provided an example of tools or techniques used in program activities.
Updated the naming convention for program management performance domains.	Updates done to language and labels used to describe program management principles and performance domains. Program management performance domains: • Strategic Alignment • Governance Framework • Benefits Management • Collaboration • Stakeholder Engagement • Life Cycle Management

X2.3.2 PROGRAM MANAGEMENT CONTENT

The Standard for Program Management—Fifth Edition presents concepts and practices unique to program management and does not imitate, copy, or represent concepts or processes that are easily referenced in the vast body of project management literature. Where program management processes rely on or may be performed similarly to those found in the project management domain, the user is directed to documentation and relevant readings in project management.

X2.3.3 BUILDING ON THE PREVIOUS EDITIONS

Valuable information and concepts were presented in earlier editions of *The Standard for Program Management*, and although there are many opportunities for improvement, the revision committee found important content and key concepts that were brought forward to the fifth edition in entirety. The team worked toward streamlining the content and presenting the information in a clear and succinct manner for users while promoting alignment across various PMI standards. By reviewing and adjudicating hundreds of written comments requesting changes, the update committee ensured the valuable elements of previous editions were woven into the framework of the update.

X2.4 OVERVIEW OF SECTIONS

Based on the objectives of the update team and the approach approved by PMI, the format and layout of the standard evolved into sections that cover program management principles, program management performance domains, and supportive text classified as program activities. These have been presented as separate and distinct sections bound in one standard. This approach was validated through the committee's discussions, references to other global program management standards, and critically important literature about program management. The resulting output and framework can now be summarized in the graphics and explanations that follow. A high-level view of the framework for the fifth edition illustrates the orientation toward principle-led performance of programs in organizations and includes discussions for each principle introduced, as well as the correlation with the performance domains. By approaching the standard in this way, each section contributes to the content of the document as a complete thought; yet each is an integral component of the whole, tying and linking the standard together from the initial section through the glossary. At the highest level, the framework for the fifth edition is illustrated in Table X2-2.

Sections X2.4.1 through X2.4.4 describe each section of the fifth edition of the standard and detail the changes the reader will find when comparing earlier editions.

Table X2-2. Overview of Framework for Fifth Edition

The Standard for Program Management—Fifth Edition	
High-Level Layout Framework	
Section 1	Introduction
Section 2	Program Management Principles
Section 3	Program Management Performance Domains
Section 4	Program Activities
Appendices	Appendix X1: Program Activities, Tools, and Techniques
	Appendix X2: Fifth Edition Changes
	Appendix X3: Contributors and Reviewers of The Standard for Program Management
References	
Glossary	
Index	

X2.4.1 SECTION 1: INTRODUCTION

Changes were made throughout Section 1 to improve consistency within the standard and ensure that key concepts covered in Sections 2 through 4 were introduced early in the document.

In Section 1.1, the meaning of principles was expanded to align with the new section on principles and give guidance for use in practice.

In Section 1.2, the possibility of programs being initiated inside portfolios, or where portfolios may not exist, was introduced. Further scenarios of structuring programs, projects, and portfolios as components for value delivery have been introduced, and figures illustrating examples have been updated.

Content from Section 1.4 of the fourth edition, which addressed the differences and interactions between program management and project management in detail, was removed and identified for inclusion in PMIstandards+®. Sections 1.5 through 1.9 were subsequently renumbered to 1.4 through 1.8.

In Section 1.5, the reference to business value was updated to organizational value. Content from the fourth edition's Sections 2.4 and 2.5 was absorbed into Section 1 to keep the introductory content that is applicable to program management in one section. Section 1.10.3 on complexity has been simplified and presented in a tabular format.

As with previous editions, an effort was made to harmonize this section with other PMI foundational standards. Table X2-3 outlines the revised Section 1.

Table X2-3. Section 1 – Fifth Edition

Section 1	Introduction
1.1	Purpose of *The Standard for Program Management*
1.2	What Is a Program?
1.2.1	Initiation of Programs
1.2.2	The Relationships among Portfolios, Programs, Operations, and Projects
1.3	What Is Program Management?
1.4	The Relationships among Organizational Strategy, Program Management, Portfolio Management, and Operations Management
1.5	Organizational Business Value
1.6	Role of the Program Manager
1.6.1	Program Manager Competencies
1.7	Role of the Program Sponsor
1.8	Role of the Program Management Office
1.9	Program and Project Distinctions
1.9.1	Uncertainty
1.9.2	Managing Change
1.9.3	Complexity
1.10	Portfolio and Program Distinctions

X2.4.2 SECTION 2: PROGRAM MANAGEMENT PRINCIPLES

Section 2 presents updated information on the principles of program management that serve as foundational guidelines for program managers. Table X2-4 shows the content of the new fifth edition's Section 2.

Table X2-4. Section 2 – Fifth Edition

Section 2	Program Management Principles
2.1	Stakeholders
2.2	Benefits Realization
2.3	Synergy
2.4	Team of Teams
2.5	Change
2.6	Leadership
2.7	Risk
2.8	Governance

X2.4.3 SECTION 3: PROGRAM MANAGEMENT PERFORMANCE DOMAINS

Section 3 of the fifth edition was previously Section 2 in earlier editions. This section has now transitioned to only discuss the program management performance domains and their characteristics. Sections 2.4 and 2.5 in the fourth edition have been moved into Section 1 as Sections 1.9 and 1.10, respectively. Section 2.3 in the fourth edition was removed and identified for use in more dynamic content formats such as PMIstandards+®.

This new Section 3 has been expanded to incorporate all program management performance domains and content in one section to support logical flow and streamlining of the standard.

A new program management performance domain called Collaboration has been introduced as Section 3.7. Collaboration has been identified as underlying—and interacting with—all other performance domains and is integral to program management.

Summary graphic Figure 3-1 in the standard demonstrates the interactions of the program management performance domains and has been updated to incorporate the Collaboration performance domain. Refer to Table X2-5 for an overview of Section 3.

Table X2-5. Section 3 – Fifth Edition

Section 3	Program Management Performance Domains
3.1	Program Management Performance Domain Definitions
3.2	Program Management Performance Domain Interactions
3.3	Strategic Alignment
3.4	Benefits Management
3.5	Stakeholder Engagement
3.6	Governance Framework
3.7	Collaboration
3.8	Life Cycle Management

X2.4.4 SECTION 3.3: STRATEGIC ALIGNMENT

The former Program Strategy Alignment performance domain, previously Section 3 in the fourth edition, was revised to Section 3.3 and its name was updated to Strategic Alignment. The content was reviewed to remove specific examples that were not applicable to all types of programs. Specific details of types and examples of environmental analyses have been removed and kept as a high-level, illustrative list as follows: comparative advantage analysis, feasibility studies, SWOT (strengths, weaknesses, opportunities, and threats) analysis, assumptions analysis, and historical information analysis.

This section maintains high-level details of program risk management strategy as a means for ensuring the program is aligned with organizational strategy.

Other changes were minor and included updating graphics and adding concluding summary paragraphs that describe the interactions with other program management performance domains and principles. Table X2-6 shows the content of Section 3.3 in the fifth edition.

Table X2-6. Section 3.3 – Fifth Edition

Section 3.3	Strategic Alignment
3.3.1	Program Business Case
3.3.2	Program Charter
3.3.3	Program Management Plan
3.3.4	Environmental Assessments
3.3.4.1	Enterprise Environmental Factors
3.3.4.2	Environmental Analysis
3.3.5	Program Risk Management Strategy
3.3.5.1	Risk Management for Strategic Alignment
3.3.5.2	Program Risk Thresholds
3.3.5.3	Initial Program Risk Assessment
3.3.5.4	Program Risk Response Strategy
3.3.6	Interactions with Program Management Principles and Other Program Management Performance Domains

X2.4.5 SECTION 3.4: BENEFITS MANAGEMENT

Section 4 of the fourth edition became Section 3.4 in the fifth edition, and the title of the performance domain was updated to Benefits Management throughout the section and standard. The terminology was updated to align with other sections of the standard.

Other changes were minor and included adding concluding, summary paragraphs that describe the interactions with other program management principles and performance domains. Table X2-7 provides an overview of Section 3.4.

Table X2-7. Section 3.4 – Fifth Edition

Section 3.4	Benefits Management
3.4.1	**Benefits Identification**
3.4.1.1	Benefits Register
3.4.2	**Benefits Analysis and Planning**
3.4.2.1	Benefits Management Plan
3.4.2.2	Benefits Management and the Program Roadmap
3.4.2.3	Benefits Register Update
3.4.3	**Benefits Delivery**
3.4.3.1	Benefits and Program Components
3.4.3.2	Benefits and Governance Framework
3.4.4	**Benefits Transition**
3.4.5	**Benefits Sustainment**
3.4.6	**Interactions with Program Management Principles and Other Program Management Performance Domains**

X2.4.6 SECTION 3.5: STAKEHOLDER ENGAGEMENT

Program stakeholder engagement appeared in the first edition of the standard as one of the three themes in program management, along with benefits realization and governance. Stakeholder engagement was previously covered in Section 5 in the fourth edition. In the fifth edition, the content is covered in Section 3.5 and has been updated to align with the nomenclature of the Stakeholder Engagement performance domain. The changes to this section were minimal and focused on clearly highlighting the stakeholder register as an example. Concluding summary paragraphs were provided and the tables and figures were updated. Table X2-8 provides an overview of Section 3.5.

Table X2-8. Section 3.5 – Fifth Edition

Section 3.5	Stakeholder Engagement
3.5.1	Program Stakeholder Identification
3.5.2	Program Stakeholder Analysis
3.5.3	Program Stakeholder Engagement Planning
3.5.4	Program Stakeholder Engagement
3.5.5	Program Stakeholder Communications
3.5.6	Interactions with Program Management Principles and Other Program Management Performance Domains

X2.4.7 SECTION 3.6: GOVERNANCE FRAMEWORK

Program governance appeared in the first edition of the standard and was covered in Section 6 of the fourth edition. In the fifth edition, the content has migrated to Section 3.6 and updates have been made to incorporate the introduction of the Governance program management principle. The nomenclature of the performance domain has been updated to Governance Framework, which allows a clear distinction from the Governance program management principle. The terms used in the section and throughout the standard were updated to refer to the Governance Framework performance domain. Topics covered in other parts of the standard that presented as duplications were reviewed.

Where appropriate, the fifth edition continues to leverage and align with *Governance of Portfolios, Programs, and Projects: A Practice Guide* [8], covering roles and responsibilities and program and governance relationships. Content has been rearranged and streamlined to promote synchronization with other parts of the standard. Table X2-9 presents the content of Section 3.6.

Table X2-9. Section 3.6 – Fifth Edition

Section 3.6	Governance Framework
3.6.1	**Governance Framework Practices**
3.6.1.1	Program Governance Plan
3.6.1.2	Governance Framework and Organizational Vision and Goals
3.6.1.3	Program Approval, Endorsement, and Definition
3.6.1.4	Program Monitoring, Reporting, and Controlling
3.6.1.5	Program Risk and Issue Governance
3.6.1.6	Program Quality Governance
3.6.1.7	Program Change Governance
3.6.1.8	Governance Framework Reviews
3.6.1.9	Program Component Initiation and Transition
3.6.1.10	Program Closure
3.6.2	**Governance Framework Roles**
3.6.2.1	Program Sponsor
3.6.2.2	Program Steering Committee
3.6.2.3	Program Management Office
3.6.2.4	Program Manager
3.6.2.5	Project Manager(s)
3.6.2.6	Other Stakeholders
3.6.3	**Governance Framework Design and Implementation**
3.6.4	**Interactions with Program Management Principles and Other Program Management Performance Domains**

X2.4.8 SECTION 3.7: COLLABORATION

Collaboration is newly introduced to the fifth edition as the sixth program management performance domain. This performance domain has risen in importance to program managers and interacts with all other performance domains integral to optimal delivery of value and benefits in programs. Collaboration addresses activities and functions geared toward generating synergy across the multiple program components.

Collaboration is covered in Section 3.7 of the standard. Table X2-10 outlines the new Section 3.7.

Table X2-10. Section 3.7 – Fifth Edition

Section 3.7	Collaboration
3.7.1	**Collaboration Factors Impacting Program Success**
3.7.1.1	Engagement
3.7.1.2	Alignment
3.7.1.3	Complexity
3.7.1.4	Transparency
3.7.1.5	Consultation
3.7.1.6	Culture
3.7.1.7	Empathy
3.7.2	**Collaboration for Benefits and Value Delivery Planning**
3.7.3	**Program Components and Activities Collaboration**
3.7.4	**Interactions with Program Management Principles and Other Program Management Performance Domains**

X2.4.9 SECTION 3.8: LIFE CYCLE MANAGEMENT

The fourth edition covered program life cycle management in Section 7. In the fifth edition, the majority of the content has been moved to Section 3.8. The section has been updated to the Life Cycle Management performance domain, and content relating to program activities, specifically program integration management, identified as a core program activity, has been moved to Section 4.

Content in this section was streamlined to remove prescriptive examples and superfluous text covered in other sections. The illustration of program life cycle phases was refreshed to allow easier understanding and demonstration of the concept. Table X2-11 provides an overview of Section 3.8.

Table X2-11. Section 3.8 – Fifth Edition

Section 3.8	Life Cycle Management
3.8.1	Program Definition Phase
3.8.1.1	Program Formulation
3.8.1.2	Program Planning
3.8.2	Program Delivery Phase
3.8.2.1	Component Authorization and Planning
3.8.2.2	Component Oversight and Integration
3.8.2.3	Component Transition and Closure
3.8.3	Program Closure Phase
3.8.4	Interactions with Program Management Principles and Other Program Management Performance Domains

X2.4.10 SECTION 4: PROGRAM ACTIVITIES

The fourth edition aligned Section 8 with Section 7 by restructuring the material into program life cycle phases and describing the activities that support each phase. In the fifth edition, this content has been brought together with integration management activities in Section 4. The section now contains the core and supporting activities that are all-encompassing of content that builds on the program management principles and performance domains.

Examples of tools and techniques applied during the program activities at various phases of the program life cycle were removed and kept in the appendix for ease of reference by users. This update serves to support the use of the standard requirements by all types, methodologies, and approaches of program management. Table X2-12 provides an overview of Section 4.

Table X2-12. Section 4 – Fifth Edition

Section 4	Program Activities
4.1	**Program Integration Management**
4.1.1	Program Integration Management Activities
4.1.2	Mapping of the Program Life Cycle to Program Activities
4.2	**Program Definition Phase Activities**
4.2.1	Program Formulation Activities
4.2.2	Program Planning Phase Activities
4.3	**Program Delivery Phase Activities**
4.3.1	Program Delivery Management
4.3.2	Program Performance Management
4.3.3	Benefits Sustainment and Program Transition
4.3.4	Program Change Management
4.3.5	Program Communications Management
4.3.6	Program Financial Management
4.3.7	Program Information Management
4.3.7.1	Lessons Learned
4.3.8	Program Procurement Management
4.3.9	Program Quality Assurance and Control
4.3.10	Program Resource Management
4.3.11	Program Risk Management
4.3.12	Program Schedule Management
4.3.13	Program Scope Management
4.4	**Program Closure Phase Activities**
4.4.1	Program Closeout
4.4.2	Program Financial Closure
4.4.3	Program Information Archiving and Transition
4.4.4	Program Procurement Closure
4.4.5	Program Resource Transition
4.4.6	Program Risk Management Transition

X2.4.11 APPENDIX X1

Appendix X1 is newly introduced to the fifth edition as a repository of examples of tools and techniques used in program activities and applied at various phases of the program life cycle. In the fourth edition, this content was part of Sections 7 or 8 and captured under integration management activities or various supporting activities of a program life cycle. These have been removed from the substantive sections of the standard and kept in the appendix for ease of reference by users. This update serves to support the design and layout of the standard into program management principles, program management performance domains, and program activities. This streamlined approach also keeps examples not applicable by all types, methodologies, and approaches of program management separate from the standard requirements. Table X2-13 provides an overview of the content in Appendix X1.

Table X2-13. Appendix X1 – Fifth Edition

Appendix X1	Program Activities, Tools, and Techniques
X1.1	Program Infrastructure Development
X1.2	Program Change Assessment
X1.3	Program Communications Assessment
X1.4	Program Initial Cost Estimation
X1.5	Program Information Management Assessment
X1.6	Program Procurement Assessment
X1.7	Program Quality Assessment
X1.8	Program Resource Requirements Estimation
X1.9	Program Initial Risk Assessment
X1.10	Program Schedule Assessment
X1.11	Program Scope Assessment
X1.12	Program Change Management Planning
X1.13	Program Communications Management Planning
X1.14	Program Cost Estimation
X1.15	Program Financial Framework Establishment
X1.16	Program Financial Management Planning
X1.17	Program Procurement Management Planning
X1.18	Program Quality Management Planning
X1.19	Program Resource Management Planning
X1.20	Program Risk Management Planning
X1.21	Program Schedule Management Planning
X1.22	Program Scope Management Planning
X1.23	Program Reporting
X1.24	Program Cost Budgeting
X1.25	Component Cost Estimation

Appendix X3
Contributors and Reviewers of *The Standard for Program Management*

The Project Management Institute is grateful to all of the contributors for their support and acknowledges their outstanding contributions to the project management profession.

X3.1 CONTRIBUTORS

The following list of contributors had input into shaping the content of the standard. Individuals listed in bold served on the Fifth Edition Development Team and individuals listed in italics served on the Fifth Edition Review Team. Inclusion of an individual's name in this list does not represent their approval or endorsement of the final content in all its parts.

Nick Clemens, PMI-ACP, PMP, Development Co-Lead
Joanna Newman, Development Co-Lead
Shyamprakash K. Agrawal, PMP, PgMP
Emad E. Aziz, PMP, PgMP, PfMP
John D. Driessnack, CSM, PMP, PfMP
Asad Ullah Chaudhry
Zhenghong Chen, MBA, MSP, PgMP
Ahmed Kamel Ghanem, PMI-ACP, DASSM, PMP
Hiroshi (Henry) Kondo, PMP, PgMP, PfMP
Muhammad U. Siddiqi, PMP, PgMP, PfMP
Essowe Abalo
Habeeb Abdulla, MS, CSM, PMP
Hamidur Rahman Adnan, PMP, PgMP, PfMP
Satishkumar Agrawal, SPC, PMP, PgMP
Phill Akinwale, OPM3, PMI-ACP, PMP
Emi Akiode, PMP
Ramy Saeed Alghamdi
Stephen Ali
Hammam (Marshal) Alkouz

Muhannad Ali Almarzooq
Gehad Ali Almassabi, PMI-ACP, PMP, PgMP
Délio Almeida, PMI-RMP, PMP
Sara Alnasser
Fatima Awwad Alrowaili
Riyad AlMallak
Hanan AlMaziad, MSC, PMP, PgMP, PfMP
Amir K Al-Nizami, PhD, MPM, PMP
Tamim A. Alsunidi, PMP
Wael (Lilo) Altali, MPA, CBAP, PMP
Abdulrahman Alulaiyan, MBA, PfMP
Nahlah Alyamani, PMI-ACP, PMP, PgMP
Ashwani Anant, PMI-ACP, PMI-RMP, PMP
Sathya Andivel, CMA, PMP, PgMP
Kenichiro Aratake, PMP
Serajul Arfeen, PMI-ACP, PMP, PgMP
Humberto Arias
Alfredo Armijos, PMO-CP, PMI-RMP, PMP
Khalid Ibraheem Asiri, PMI-RMP, PMP
Mohammed Azmy Ateia
Sivaram Athmakuri, PMI-ACP, PMI-PBA, PMP

Vahid Azadmanesh, DBA, PMP, PfMP

Akbar Azwir, PMI-CC, Prosci CCP, PMP

Claudia M. Baca

Pierre Beaudry, Jr., C.ADM, MGP, PMP

Nasrin Beikzand

T. A. Best, PMP

Nico Beylemans

Mohammed Saleh Bin Askar, PMP, PgMP, PfMP

Nigel Blampied, PhD, PE, PMP

Greta Blash, PMI-RMP, PMP, PgMP

Kiron Bondale, PMI-ACP, PMI-RMP, PMP

Bedanga Bordoloi

Felipe Moraes Borges, PMO-CP

Miguel A. Botana Cobas, MBA, PMP

Adrian Bottomley, PMP, PgMP, PfMP

Damiano Bragantini, PMP

Ellie Braham, RIMS-CRMP, ATP, PMP

Larkland Brown

Sathish Kumar C

Leandro Maximiliano Cabani

Feren Calderwood, GSLC, PMP

Heberth Campos, PMI-ACP, PMI-RMP, PMP

James F. Carilli, PhD, PMP, PgMP

Iqbal Cassim

José Cascante Cespedes

S. Chandramouli, PhD, PfMP

V. Paul C. Charlesraj, MS, MRICS, PMP

Porfirio Chen Chang

Alexandra Chapman

Panos Chatzipanos, PhD, WRE, Dr Eur Ing

Nguyen Si Trieu Chau, PMP, PgMP, PfMP

Antonio Checa

David A. Chigne, PMI-ACP, PMI-RMP, PMP

John Peter D

Gina Davidovic, PMP, PgMP

Deanna E. Davies, MBA, PMP

Jinky T. Dela Torre, MBA, PMP

Luke Desmond

Saju Devassy

Gaurav Dhooper, PAL-I, CSAPM, PMI-ACP

Cynthia Dionisio

Danil Dintsis, PMP, PgMP, PfMP

Louisa Dixon

Michael Doherty

Esha Doshi, PMP

Michael Doyle

Darya Duma

Troy Edelen, CCMP, DASM, PMP

Sylvie Edwards

Hussameldeen Elhaw

Wael K. Elmetwaly

Nabeel Eltyeb, MoP, P3O, PMP

Jose Daniel Esterkin

Srinivas Reddy Eticala

Ahmed Ali Eziza, Eng, IPMO-E, PMP

Puian Masudi Far, PhD, PMP

Jane M. Farley, CMC, CMInstD, PMP

Jean-Luc Favrot, PMI-ACP, DASSM, PMP

Amr Fayez, SFC, SSYB, PMP

Piotr Felcenloben

Rieski Ferdian, PMP

Leana Fischer, PgMP

Mitchell R. Fong, P.Eng, DAC, PMP

Ali Forouzesh, PhDc, OPM3, PfMP

Luis Eduardo França

Iain Fraser, PMP, PMI Fellow

Carlos Augusto Freitas, DAC, DASSM, PMP

Yuhang Fu

Marius Gaitan, Eng, PMI-PBA, PMP

Diego Galárraga

Abhijit Ganguly, PMI-ACP, PMP, PgMP

Edwardo Garcia, PhD

Jason Gardel

Ashutosh Garg, PMP, PgMP, PfMP

Stanisław Gasik, PhD, PMP

Subhajit Ghosh, PMI-ACP, PMP, PgMP

Nguyen Tuan Le Giang, PMP, PgMP, PfMP

Theofanis Giotis, MSc, PhDc, PMP

Herbert G. Gonder, PMI-ACP, PMP

Dr Sumit Goyal

Scott M. Graffius

Filip Gudelj

Anil Guvenatam, PMI-ACP, PMP

Danny Ha, CISSP, FCRP, ISO Member

Mustafa Hafizoglu, PhDc, PMP

Nagy Hamamo, MB, PMP

Shahul Hameed

Maged Farouk Hanna, PhD, PMP, PfMP

Mohammed Majharul Haque, DAVSC, PgMP, PfMP

Keiko Hara, PMP

Jeff A. Harris, PMP

Lt Col L Shri Harshna, DASSM, PMP, PgMP

Gabrielle Bonin Haskins, PMP
Hironori Hayashi
Pierre Hnoud
Ivan Ho, MBA, PMI-ACP, PMP
Stephen Hollander, MBA, PMP, PgMP
Regina Holzinger, PMP
James E. Houston, IV, PE, CCM, PMP
Tarik Al Hraki, MIB, PMI-RMP, PMP
Zayar Htun, PMP
Shuichi Ikeda, CBAP, PMP
Muhammad A. B. Ilyas, PMP, PgMP
Hiroki Itakura, CSM, PMI-ACP, PMP
Mohit Jain
Md Javeed, PMP
Jean-Michel De Jaeger, EMBA, PMP
Kris Jennes, MSc, PMP
Xiang Jin
Arthur Jones-Dove
Joseph Jordan, PMP
Leo Jurgens, MPM, PMI-PBA, PMP
Ganesh K
Rami Kaibni, CBAP, PgMP, PfMP
Miki Kaneko, PMP
Gernot Kapteina, MBA, PMP, PgMP
Stylianos Kazakeos
Claude El Nakhl Khalil, PharmD, MBA, PMP
Danny Klima
Jerome Knysh
Dimitrios Kopsidas
Maciej Koszykowski, PMI-RMP, PMP, PgMP
Olena Kovalova
Wendy Kraly, MBA, PMP
Jiri Kratky
Laszlo J. Kremmer, MBA, CLC, PMP
Rajashekar Krishnaraj, PMI-RMP, PMP, PgMP
Harisha Ranganath Lakkavalli, PMP, PgMP, PfMP
Chia-Kuang Lee, CQRM, P.Tech, PMP
Wooyeon Lee, PhD, PE, PMP
Adeel Khan Leghari, PMP, PgMP
Raman Lemtsiuhou, KMP, PSM2, PMP
Uladzimir Liashchynski
Kan Lin
Tong (James) Liu, PhD, ASEP, PMP
Roberto Lofaro
Enid T. Vargas Maldonado, PhD, PMI-ACP, PMP
Rich Maltzman, PMP

Arun Mandalika
M V Rasa Manikkam, PMP
Ricardo Sastre Martín
Giampaolo Marucci, Dott., PMI-ACP, PMP
Faraz Masood, PMP
Marco Mayer
Robert McMartin
Ray Mead, MBA, PMP
Kentaro Midorikawa, PMP
Akiyoshi Miki, PMP
Kenyi Mitsuta, PMI-RMP, PMP
Walla Siddig Elhadey Mohamed, PMI-RMP,
    PMP, PgMP
Abdalla Yassin Abdalla Mohammed
Mansoor Mohammed
Alexandre Morissette, BSc, L6σ GB/Lean
    Enterprise Certified, PMP
Amr Fayez Moustafa
C Muchuchuti
Nitin Mukesh, CSM, PMP
Mohammed Muneeb, PMP, PgMP, PfMP
Muktesh Murthy
Syed Ahsan Mustaqeem, PE, PMP
Ahmed Nabil, Eng, PhD, PMP
Brijesh Nair, CEng, PMP, PgMP
Asaya Nakasone, PMP
Hiromi Nakatani
Anil Kumar Narayanan, PMP, PgMP
Faiq Nasibov, PMP
Laura Lazzerini Neuwirth, AHPP, AgilePgM, PMP
Gundo Nevhutalu, MSc, PMP
Nnogge Lovis Nkede, PMP, PgMP, PfMP
Jose Ignacio Noguera
Ranjit Oberai, PMP, PgMP, PfMP
Habeeb Omar, MBA, DASSM, PfMP
Arivazhagan Ondiappan, PMI-RMP, PMI-SP, PMP
Yuriy Oryeshkin
Carlos Singh Ospina, PMP, PgMP, PfMP
Chriss Oussama, PMP
Yoshihisa Ozaki, PMP, PgMP, PfMP
Jorge Palomino Garcia, Eng, MBA
Claude Palmarini, AHPP, SAFe Agilist, PMP
Sameer Kumar Panda, SAFe5 Agilist, PMP, PgMP
Luke Panezich, DASSM, DAVSC, PMP
François Paquin, MPM, MBA
Seenivasan Pavanasam

Mary M. Piecewicz, MBA, MSPC, PMP
Nicholas Pisano
B K Subramanya Prasad, CSM, PMP
Adi Prasetyo, PRINCE2, IPMA Level-A, PMP
Arief Prasetyo, PMI-RMP, PMP
Zulfiqar Ali Qaimkhani, PMP, PgMP, PfMP
Sami Hakam Qasim
S. Ramani, P3M3 Assessor, PgMP, PfMP
Muhammad Mohsin Rashid, PMI-ACP,
   PMI-RMP, PMP
Sagar Ashok Raut, PMI-RMP, PMP, PgMP
P. Ravikumar, PMP, PgMP, PfMP
Krupakara Reddy, PRINCE2,
   CMMI Associate, PMP
Nabeel Ur Rehman, DAVSC, PMP, PgMP
Tashfeen Riaz, DAVSC, PMP, PgMP
Dan Stelian Roman, CSSBB, PMP-ACP, PMP
Sachlani, P3OF, PSM I, PMP
Laura Sailar, PMI-ACP, PMP
Narendra Saini
Ryosuke Sako, PMP
Omar Samaniego, PMI-RMP, PMP
Abdul Raheem Samee, PMI-PBA, PMP, PgMP
Parthasarathy Sampath, CISA, PMI-RMP, PMP
Anuja Sasidharan
Toshitaka Sato, PMI-ACP, PMP, PgMP
NIna Scarnici
Gregor Schedlbauer
Mónika Toro Serrano, MSc, P.Eng, PMP
P. Seshan, PMI-ACP, PMI-RMP, PMP
Tahir Shah
Rabbani Basha Shaik, PMP, PgMP, PfMP
Nitin Shende, SPC 6, PMI-PBA, PMP
Toshiki Shimoike, PhD, PMP
Andrew Schuster, DBA, MBA, PMP
Gary Sikma, PMI-ACP, PMP
Abel Herrera Sillas, DM, PMP
Carlos Singh, PMP, PgMP, PfMP
Dharam Singh, PMP, PgMP, PfMP
Sumit Kumar Sinha
Aung Kyaw Sint, PMI-ACP, PMP, PgMP
Allen Smolinski
Josephina Solakova
Islam Mohmamed Soliman, PMI-ACP, PMP
Ping Song
Mauro Sotille, PMI-RMP, PMP

Fernando Souza, MSc, PMI-ACP, PMP
Maricarmen Suarez, PMI-ACP, PMP, PgMP
Alaa Sultan
Zdenek Svecar, A-CSM, PMP
Ernie Szeto, MSc, PMP
Tetsuya Tani, CBAP, PMP
Awadalsaid Tara
Michel Thiry, PhD, PMI Fellow
Sal J. Thompson, MBA, CSM, PMP
Claudia A. Tocantins, MSc, PMP
Süleyman Tosun, PhD, ITIL, PMP
Galen Townson, EMBA, DAVSC, PMP
Syed Waqar Uddin
Sujith Muraleedharan Ullattil, CSPO, PMP, PgMP
Terunori Umezawa, PMP
Kailash D. Upadhyay
Shibu Valsalan, PMI-ACP, PMI-PBA, PMP
Tom Van Medegael, PMI-ACP, PMP
Ravi Vanukuru, BE, PMP
Mackenzie D. Varvil
Charu Vebkataraman
Rajkumar Veera
Thierry Verlynde, CPC, PMP
Tiziano Villa, PMI-ACP, DASSM, PMP
Esteban Villegas, PMI-ACP, PMP, PgMP
David Violette, MPM
Lislal Viswam, MSc, PMO CP, PMP
Dileep Viswanathan
Harinath Vobblisetty
Thomas Walenta
Irshad Wani
Toshiyuki Watanabe
Michal Wieteska, ASEP, PMP
Brian Williamson, EdD, PgMP, PfMP
Rebecca A. Winston
Dirk Withake, PMP, PgMP, PfMP
Thomas Witterholt, PMP, PgMP
Stephan Wohlfahrt, PMI-ACP, DAVSC, PMP
Juanita M. Woods, PhD, PMP, PgMP
Te Wu
Hany I Zahran
Daniel Alfredo Zamudio López, DAC, PMP, PgMP
Stefano Mario Zanantoni
Al Zeitoun, PhD, PgMP, PMI Fellow
Eire Emilio Zimmermann
Marcin Zmigrodzki

X3.2 STAFF

Special mention is due to the following PMI employees:

Warren Duffie

Tzarmallah Haynes-Joseph, MSc

Kristin Hodgson, CAE, CSPO

Leah Huf

Christie McDevitt, APR

Josh Parrott, MBI

Kim Shinners

References

[1] Project Management Institute (PMI). (2021). *A Guide to the Project Management Body of Knowledge (PMBOK® Guide)*—Seventh Edition. PMI.

[2] Project Management Institute (PMI). (2022). *Process Groups: A Practice Guide.* PMI.

[3] Project Management Institute (PMI). (2017). *The Standard for Portfolio Management*—Fourth Edition. PMI.

[4] Project Management Institute (PMI). (2019). *The Standard for Earned Value Management.* PMI.

[5] Project Management Institute (PMI). (2017). *The Standard for Organizational Project Management (OPM).* PMI.

[6] Project Management Institute (PMI). (2019). *The Standard for Risk Management in Portfolios, Programs, and Projects.* PMI.

[7] Project Management Institute (PMI). (2017). *PMI Lexicon of Project Management Terms.* http://www.pmi.org/lexiconterms

[8] Project Management Institute (PMI). (2016). *Governance of Portfolios, Programs, and Projects: A Practice Guide.* PMI.

[9] Project Management Institute (PMI). (2017). *The Standard for Business Analysis.* PMI.

[10] Project Management Institute (PMI). (2019). *Benefits Realization Management: A Practice Guide.* PMI.

[11] Project Management Institute (PMI). (2016). *PMI Code of Ethics and Professional Conduct.* http://www.pmi.org/codeofethics

[12] Project Management Institute (PMI). (2013). *Managing Change in Organizations: A Practice Guide*. PMI.

[13] Project Management Institute (PMI). (2017). *Project Manager Competency Development Framework*—Third Edition. PMI.

[14] Project Management Institute (PMI). (2014). *Navigating Complexity: A Practice Guide.* PMI.

[15] Ambler, S. W., & Lines, M. (2022). *Choose Your WoW! A Disciplined Agile Approach to Optimizing Your Way of Working.* Project Management Institute (PMI).

[16] Project Management Institute (PMI). (2019). *Practice Standard for Scheduling* —Third Edition. PMI.

Glossary

INCLUSIONS AND EXCLUSIONS

This glossary includes terms that are:

▶ Unique to program management (e.g., benefits management); and

▶ Not unique to program management, but used differently or with a narrower meaning in program management than in general everyday usage (e.g., benefit, risk).

This glossary generally does not include:

▶ Application- or industry-specific terms;

▶ Terms used in program management that do not differ in any material way from everyday use (e.g., business outcome); or

▶ Terms used in program management that do not differ from a similar term defined in the *PMBOK® Guide*—Seventh Edition, except that these terms are now used at a program level instead of a project level (e.g., a program charter and a project charter both serve the same purpose—to approve the start of the effort).

DEFINITIONS

Many of the words defined in this glossary may have broader and, in some cases, different dictionary definitions to accommodate the context of program management.

Benefit. The gains and assets realized by the organization and other stakeholders as the result of outcomes delivered by the program.

Benefits Analysis and Planning Phase. Establishes the program benefits management plan and develops the benefits metrics and framework for monitoring and controlling both the components and the measurement of benefits within the program.

Benefits Delivery Phase. Ensures that the program delivers the expected benefits, as defined in the benefits management plan.

Benefits Identification Phase. Analyzes the available information about organizational and business strategies, internal and external influences, and program drivers to identify and quantify the benefits that program stakeholders expect to realize.

Benefits Management. Processes that clarify the program's planned benefits and intended outcomes and includes processes for monitoring the program's ability to deliver against these benefits and outcomes.

Benefits Management Performance Domain. Performance domain that defines, creates, maximizes, and delivers the benefits provided by the program.

Benefits Management Plan. The documented explanation defining the processes for creating, optimizing, and sustaining the benefits provided by a project or program.

Benefits Sustainment Phase. Ongoing program maintenance activities sometimes performed beyond the end of the program by receiving organizations to assure continued generation of the improvements and outcomes delivered by the program.

Benefits Transition Phase. Program activities that ensure that benefits are transitioned to operational areas and can be sustained once they are transferred.

Business Case. A documented economic feasibility study used to establish validity of the benefits to be delivered by a program.

Collaboration Performance Domain. Performance domain that creates and maintains synergy across stakeholders, both internal and external, to optimize benefits delivery and realization.

Component. Related activities conducted to support a program.

Constraint. A factor that limits the options for managing a project, program, portfolio, or process.

Critical Thinking. A process in which one applies observation, analysis, inference, context, reflective thinking, and the like, in order to reach judgments. Such judgments should be open to alternative perspectives that may not normally be otherwise considered.

Customer Operating Organization. The organization that receives or is willing to pay for the outputs, outcomes, and/or benefits delivered by the performing organization.

Delivery Organization. The performing organization, collectively with all its subcontractors and affiliates, are referred to as the delivery organization.

Enterprise Environmental Factors (EEFs). Conditions, not under the immediate control of the team, that influence, constrain, or direct the project, program, or portfolio.

Governance Framework Performance Domain. Performance domain that enables and performs program decision-making, establishes practices to support the program, and maintains program oversight.

Intangible (or Nontangible) Benefits. Benefits that are intended for a program to produce but cannot be measured in units of money.

Life Cycle Management. Managing all program activities related to program definition, program delivery, and program closure.

Life Cycle Management Performance Domain. Performance domain that manages program activities required to facilitate effective program definition, program delivery, and program closure.

Operating Organization. The organization(s) responsible for operating the output(s) of the program and sustaining and optimizing the benefits realization resulting from such outputs.

Performing Organization. An enterprise whose personnel are the most directly involved in doing the work of the project or program.

Phase Gate. A review at the end of a phase in which a decision is made to continue to the next phase, to continue with modification, or to end a project or program.

Portfolio. Projects, programs, subsidiary portfolios, and operations managed as a group to achieve strategic objectives. See also *program* and *project*.

Portfolio Management. The centralized management of one or more portfolios to achieve strategic objectives. See also *program management* and *project management*.

Portfolio Manager. The person or group assigned by the performing organization to establish, balance, monitor, and control portfolio components in order to achieve strategic business objectives. See also *program manager* and *project manager*.

Procurement Management Plan. A component of the project or program management plan that describes how a team will acquire goods and services from outside of the performing organization.

Program. Related projects, subsidiary programs, and program activities managed in a coordinated manner to obtain benefits not available from managing them individually. See also *portfolio* and *project*.

Program Activities. Tasks and work conducted to support a program and which contribute throughout the program life cycle.

Program Change Management. Activities to plan for, monitor, control, and administer changes during the course of the program.

Program Charter. A document issued by a sponsor that authorizes the program management team to use organizational resources to execute the program and links the program to the organization's strategic objectives.

Program Closure Phase. Program activities necessary to retire or transition program benefits to a sustaining organization and formally close the program in a controlled manner.

Program Communications Management. Activities necessary for the timely and appropriate generation, collection, distribution, storage, retrieval, and ultimate disposition of program information.

Program Definition Phase. Program activities conducted to authorize the program and develop the program management plan or roadmap required to achieve the expected results.

Program Delivery Phase. Program activities performed to produce the intended results of each component in accordance with the program management plan or roadmap.

Program Financial Framework. A high-level initial plan for coordinating available funding, determining constraints, and determining how funding is allocated.

Program Financial Management. Activities related to identifying the program's financial sources and resources, integrating the budgets of the program components, developing the overall budget for the program, and controlling costs during the program.

Program Governance Plan. A document that describes the systems and methods to be used to monitor, manage, and support a given program, and the responsibilities of specific roles for ensuring the timely and effective use of those systems and methods. A program governance plan is sometimes subsumed into the program management plan.

Program Information Management. Activities related to how the program's information assets are prepared, collected, organized, and secured.

Program Information Management Plan. A component of the program management plan that describes how the program's information assets will be prepared, collected, and organized.

Program Integration Management. Program activities conducted to identify, define, combine, unify, and coordinate multiple components into the program.

Program Management. The application of knowledge, skills, and principles to a program to achieve the program objectives and to obtain benefits and control not available by managing program components individually. See also *portfolio management* and *project management*.

Program Management Information System. Tools used to collect, integrate, and communicate information critical for the effective management of one or more organizational programs.

Program Management Office. A management structure that standardizes the program-related governance processes and facilitates the sharing of resources, methodologies, tools, and techniques.

Program Management Performance Domain. Complementary groupings of related areas of activity or function that uniquely characterize and differentiate the activities found in one performance domain from the others within the full scope of program management work.

Program Management Plan. A document that integrates the program's subsidiary plans and establishes the management controls and overall plan for integrating and managing the program's individual components.

Program Manager. The person authorized by the performing organization to lead the team or teams responsible for achieving program objectives.

Program Master Schedule. An output of a schedule model that logically links components, milestones, and high-level activities necessary to deliver program benefits, sometimes referred to as a program integrated master schedule.

Program Procurement Management. The application of knowledge, skills, tools, and techniques necessary to acquire products and services to meet the needs of the overall program and the constituent projects/components.

Program Quality Assurance. The activities related to the periodic evaluation of the overall program quality to provide confidence that the program will comply with relevant quality policies and standards.

Program Quality Control. The monitoring of specific components or program deliverables and results to determine if they meet the quality requirements and lead to benefits realization.

Program Quality Management. The activities of the performing organization that determine program quality policies, objectives, and responsibilities so that the program will be successful.

Program Resource Management. Program activities that ensure all required resources (people, equipment, materials, etc.) are made available to the component managers to enable the delivery of benefits for the program.

Program Risk. An uncertain event or condition that, if it occurs, has a positive or negative effect on the program.

Program Risk Management. Program activities related to actively identifying, monitoring, analyzing, accepting, mitigating, avoiding, or retiring program risk.

Program Risk Register. A document in which risks are recorded together with the results of risk analysis and risk response planning.

Program Roadmap. A chronological representation of a program's intended direction that graphically depicts dependencies between major milestones and decision points and reflects the linkage between the business strategy and the program work.

Program Schedule Management. An activity to determine the order and timing of the components needed to produce the program benefits, estimate the amount of time required to accomplish each one, identify significant milestones during the performance of the program, and document the outcomes of each milestone.

Program Scope Management. Activities that define, develop, monitor, control, and verify program scope.

Program Steering Committee. Group of participants representing various program-related interests with the purpose of supporting the program under its authority by providing guidance, endorsements, and approvals through the governance practices. This committee may also be referred to as a program governance board.

Project. A temporary endeavor undertaken to create a unique product, service, or result. See also *portfolio* and *program*.

Project Management. The application of knowledge, skills, tools, and techniques to project activities to meet the project requirements. See also *portfolio management* and *program management*.

Project Manager. The person assigned by the performing organization to lead the team that is responsible for achieving the project objectives. See also *portfolio manager* and *program manager*.

Quality Management Plan. A component of the project or program management plan that describes how an organization's policies, procedures, and guidelines will be implemented to achieve the quality objectives. See also *program management plan*.

Risk Management Plan. A component of the project, program, or portfolio management plan that describes how risk management activities will be structured and performed. See also *program management plan*.

Schedule Management Plan. A component of the project or program management plan that establishes the criteria for developing, monitoring, and controlling the schedule. See also *program management plan*.

Scope Management Plan. A component of the project or program management plan that describes how the scope will be defined, developed, monitored, controlled, and validated. See also *program management plan*.

Sponsor. An individual or a group that provides resources and support for the project, program, or portfolio, and is accountable for enabling success. See also *stakeholder*.

Stakeholder. An individual, group, or organization that may affect, be affected by, or perceive itself to be affected by a decision, activity, or outcome of a project, program, or portfolio. See also *sponsor*.

Stakeholder Engagement. Activities conducted to identify and analyze stakeholder needs and manage expectations and communications to foster stakeholder support.

Stakeholder Engagement Performance Domain. Performance domain that identifies and analyzes stakeholder needs and manages expectations and communications to foster stakeholder support.

Strategic Alignment. Activities associated with the integration and development of business strategies and organizational goals and objectives, and the degree to which operations and performance meet the stated organizational goals and objectives.

Strategic Alignment Performance Domain. Performance domain that identifies program outputs and outcomes to provide benefits aligned with the organization's goals and objectives.

Index

Benefits realization management, 44, 45

Benefits Realization Management: A Practice Guide, 1

Benefits Realization principle, 40, 43–45, 132

Benefits register, 84–85, 88

Benefits sustainment, 44, 45, 82, 94–95, 162, 232

Benefits transition, 91–93, 162, 232

Bottom-up approach to program initiation, 10

Budget, 165, 188, 198–199. *See also* Program funding

Business case, 232. *See also* Program business case

Business skills, 21, 23

Business value. *See* Value

C

Change(s)
  assessing, 179
  external, 30, 52
  governance framework of, 115
  identifying sources of, 53
  initiatives for, 30
  internal, 30, 52
  program manager and, 30, 99–100, 115
  program steering committee on, 115
  resistance to, 99
  risks related to, 30, 52, 115
  stakeholders and, 99–100, 106
Change management
  activities for, 16, 30, 155, 163, 179, 184
  complexity and, 33
  defining, 233
  effective, 51, 53
  factors of, 53
  planning, 184
  in portfolios, 52
  in programs, 30–31, 51–53
  in projects, 30, 31, 52
  skills for, 22
Change management office, 16
Change principle, 40, 51–53, 132, 133, 134
Charter. *See* Program charter
Clarity, in stakeholder engagement, 42
Closure phase. *See* Program closure phase
Cognitive-based trust, 56

Cognitive intelligence, 55

Collaboration, 129–139
  absence of, 133
  across components, 130, 138–139
  balancing, 138–139
  for benefits delivery, 135–137
  in business case development, 69
  communication in, 131, 134
  defining, 65
  factors of, 131–135
  in governance, 62, 118, 137, 138
  in portfolios, 135, 136
  in programs, 129–130
  among program team members, 107
  in projects, 129, 138
  in stakeholder engagement, 42, 131
  successful, 129, 131–135, 138
  timing of, 134
  for value delivery, 135–137
Collaboration performance domain, 129, 139, 232
Collaboration skills, 22–23, 57
Communication
  activities for, 155, 164, 179, 184–185, 198
  assessing, 179
  in collaboration, 131, 134
  skills for, 22, 24, 106, 120
  in stakeholder engagement, 97, 99, 106, 107–108
Competitive advantage, 43
Complexity
  characteristics of, 98
  collaboration and, 132–133
  defining, 31
  of portfolios, 132
  of programs, 31–33, 58, 98, 132
  of projects, 31–33, 132
  synergy and, 48
Compliance, governance and, 61
Component(s)
  authorization and planning of, 147
  change to, 30, 31, 52, 53, 89–90
  collaboration across, 130, 138–139
  defining, 6, 232
  estimating costs of, 199
  goals of, 5
  initiating, 116–117, 161
  managing, 5, 14–15, 18, 116–117, 124, 146

The Standard for Program Management

The Standard for Program Management

Risk(s) *(continued)*
  identifying, 59, 182
  initial, 182
  internal, 114
  monitoring, 169, 194
  negative, 58, 133, 182
  in portfolios, 133
  positive, 58, 86, 133, 182
  program charter and, 71
  in programs, 133
  in projects, 133
  schedule and, 196
  synergy and, 48
  tolerating, 28
  uncertainty and, 28
Risk and issue governance framework, 114
Risk assessment, 59, 77–78, 182
Risk management
  activities for, 155, 169, 174, 182, 194
  benefits realization and, 45, 58, 59, 82, 86
  defining, 235
  importance of, 58
  planning, 194, 235
  skills for, 23
  for strategic alignment, 76
  successful, 59
Risk management strategy, 68, 76–78
Risk principle, 40, 58–59, 133, 134
Risk profiles, 194
Risk register, 194, 235
Risk response strategy, 78
Risk sensitivity, 194
Risk targets, 194
Risk thresholds, 77, 78, 114, 194
Roadmap. *See* Program roadmap

S

Schedule, 169–170, 183, 195–196
Schedule management plan, 195–196, 236
Scope management plan, 170, 195, 197, 236
Scope of program, 71, 155, 170, 183, 197, 235
SEPMO. *See* Strategic enterprise project
    management office
Social intelligence, 55

SOW. *See* Statement of work
Sponsor(s), 236. *See also* Program sponsor(s)
Stakeholder(s)
  agreeing to planned benefits, 45
  analyzing, 103–104
  business case by, 69
  defining, 97, 236
  expectations of, 41, 42, 97, 106
  external, 97
  identifying, 97, 100–102
  internal, 97
  managing, 97
  mapping, 98, 103, 104
  power/interest grid and, 103–104
  program charter and, 71
  program manager and, 19, 20, 99–100, 103,
    106, 107
  register of, 100–102
  synergy and, 48
Stakeholder engagement, 97–108
  change and, 99–100, 106
  collaboration in, 42, 131
  communication in, 97, 99, 106, 107–108
  defining, 65, 236
  elements of, 98
  goal of, 97
  metrics for, 106
  planning, 105
  process of, 41–42
  as program management principle, 40, 41–42
  skills for, 20, 22
Stakeholder Engagement performance domain,
    108, 236
Stakeholder environment, 98
Stakeholder register, 100–102
Stakeholders principle, 40, 41–42, 131, 133, 134,
    135
The Standard for Business Analysis, 1
The Standard for Earned Value Management, 1,
    113
*The Standard for Organizational Project
    Management,* 1
The Standard for Portfolio Management, 1, 6, 10,
    18, 111
*The Standard for Risk Management in Portfolios,
    Programs, and Projects,* 1, 133, 194